THE
dysfunctional
WORKPLACE

From chaos to collaboration: a
guide to keeping sane on the job

Peter Morris, Radio's Business Shrink
Introduction by Peter Laufer

BUSINESS
avon, massachusetts

Published by Adams Business, an imprint of
Adams Media, an F+W Publications Company
57 Littlefield Street, Avon, MA 02322
www.adamsmedia.com

ISBN-10: 1-59869-413-8
ISBN-13: 978-1-59869-413-0

Printed in Canada.

J I H G F E D C B A

Library of Congress Cataloging-in-Publication
Data is available from the publisher.

The lyrics to "Still Ain't Satisfied" appear by
permission of Bonnie Lockhart.

This book is available at quantity discounts for
bulk purchases. For information, please call
1-800-289-0963.

contents

acknowledgments

The list is long of those I need to acknowledge for the successes of the Business Shrink radio show, Web site, blog, and—of course—this book.

Mindy Schulte was the show's founding producer; she was followed by Dan Zoll, Katrina Rill, and Ingalisa Schrobsdorff. Together my producers have been tenacious and skillful at securing the extraordinary guest list for the radio show, stars reflected in the sources you find in this book.

James Vontayes and Michelle Wiersema have been by my side since the launch of the show as associate producers. It is James Vontayes who keeps me focused in our Chicago studio—especially on the dictatorial requirements of the clock. Radio and its coconspirator time are severe taskmasters, and James makes sure I do not forget that the conversations I enjoy with guests and the audience must not linger endlessly, no matter how enjoyable and informative they may be.

Our technical director, Ken Bryant, keeps us on the air, with help from our audio engineers Jada White and Andrew Roth.

Ned Robertson is the Business Shrink art director and Chris Slattery our design director. I've been ably assisted by writers and researchers Randy Lyman, Jeff Kamen, and Marc Polonsky. James Harris is our web developer and Joel Mackey our webmaster.

The Business Shrink marketing director is Shane Hackett. Coordinating the brand is Kurt Iverson, who developed the Business Shrink social networking Web site.

My thanks to our fine transcribers Kathy Talbert and Barbara Skow.

And finally, of course, I want to thank my guests for participating in the interviews and conversations from which we learn so much, and my listeners—especially those who choose to call the show and who add just the dose of reality we need to make sure the Business Shrink is taking care of business.

about **The BUSINESS Shrink** series

Peter Laufer » Welcome to the Business Shrink series, books designed to help you navigate the often-treacherous seas of the business world. Business Shrink Peter Morris is your co-captain on your business journey. So relax. He's been across these waters dozens of times, and he's here to help make sure you make it safely to your business ports of call.

For several years now I've been privileged to work directly with Peter Morris as he's developed his nationwide radio show, launched his interactive Web site, and dipped his quill in the inkwell to put his words on paper for the Business Shrink books. I've been paying close attention as he's sparred on the air with an extraordinary cast of characters from the pantheon of business players: CEOs and entrepreneurs, business school deans, business book authors, and business news reporters. Add to that list the spectacular business questions and business stories that come from the callers and e-mailers in the radio show audience, and you can understand what a stimulating work environment it is for me to roll up my sleeves and labor in the Business Shrink's world.

It is a nonstop learning experience, and there is absolutely no question in my mind that after all those hours in the studio with Peter Morris—the two of us interpreting, pontificating, joking, and analyzing business—I've earned my MBA equivalent from the virtual Business Shrink Institute of Advanced Business Affairs. The books in this series are filled with the kind of advice and information that will provide you with the same sort of education I've enjoyed.

As the Business Shrink, Peter Morris explores the so-often-ignored reality that successful business relies on psychology and strategy. He knows successful business means problem solving. Too many people consider that business is based solely on power and logic and that it's absent feeling. At the same time they dismiss feeling as not logical and not businesslike.

In fact, this three-way intersection of business, psychology, and strategy is critical for people solving thorny problems in their business lives. The Business Shrink helps his "patients" find solutions to business problems based on this formula. From his years of experience on the frontlines of the business wars, entrepreneur Peter Morris knows how to help others find that critical balance point between logic and feeling. And he knows how and when to add an appropriate dose of power.

Brash, blunt, and loath to suffer fools gladly or otherwise, Peter Morris combines his academic and professional background (Princeton, Harvard, thirty-plus years of international real-estate adventures) with the street smarts of a cigar-chomping Chicago success story. The result is these scrappy guides to solving daily business problems.

Every week Peter Morris is on the air across America with his radio show dealing with the business-world problems of his audience members. He brings his radio problem-solving techniques to these books, teaching readers how to manage workplace problems on a daily basis, before those problems become crises. And he defines *business* in the broadest possible manner: Just about everything we do every day involves business.

Because of his years of entrepreneurial experience, Peter Morris knows the needs of the small business owner and the small business employee. He can offer effective solutions to most business problems because he's seen and dealt with most of the symptoms that plague business owners and employees. Over and over again his listeners respond to his personalized answers to their questions by thanking him and saying, "That's a great idea. I never thought of that. I'm going to try that." When he hears back from them, for follow-up treatments, more often than not his ideas worked. The Business Shrink's personality cuts through the fog of jargon and offers a straight path to solutions. Peter Morris has a clear view of the business world and of how to develop win-win scenarios. His advice is long lasting—and in these books he offers readers templates for solving future problems.

Think you have too little time and not enough money? Those concerns are usually just excuses, according to the Business Shrink, who counsels readers to step outside normal expectations and categories, and adopt his worldview. Perhaps most important, this Chicagoan has a low tolerance for self-pity. His advice is as merciless as it is productive.

Peter Morris has multiple degrees from the School of Hard Knocks, along with an undergraduate degree from Princeton University in Public Affairs and East Asian Studies, and a law degree from Harvard Law School. Over the last thirty-odd years of doing business worldwide, he has made and lost fortunes. He knows the systems. Today his primary work is as a real-estate investor and as a financial advisor for funding and merger acquisition activities. He currently owns and controls real-estate assets worldwide with a development value in excess of $1 billion. His other interests include investing in and establishing biotech and health-care companies in conjunction with Harvard University and its affiliated hospitals.

As the Business Shrink, Peter Morris enjoys the opportunity to share his expertise with the radio audience, answering questions from novices in business and analyzing the state of the business world with business experts. Peter Morris leads newcomers to business by the hand, helping them figure out their paths to success while he engages as a peer with the captains of industry, analyzing capitalism's successes and failures. Peter Morris insists that a successful business and a happy businessperson must combine right-brain and left-brain activities. He knows successful business means problem solving.

These are opinion-driven business books, but these opinions have been tested in those thirty years of real-world successful experience. Life requires some tough choices; it requires facing reality. "Get real and make sense," says the Business Shrink, "and you can solve your business problems." He teaches his readers how to get past the things that stymie and consume them, and to get on with the business of business. These are problem-solving books, designed for you to write in, dog-ear, and spill your lunch on—in other words, for you to refer to repeatedly, as problems and challenges arise within your work life.

The Business Shrink series helps readers do what Peter Morris does: reduce a crisis to a yawn. Anywhere in the business world where a reader may be mired, he's been during his long career, so his view helps the reader get past the obstacles and obtain business success.

Bon voyage!

introduction

the personality of your workplace

Is This Your Office? Are you someone who does *not* look forward to going to work? Are there people in your office who backbite and gossip? Are there people in your office who like to throw cold water on every new idea you have? Do some of your office mates try to steal your ideas when they can? Are there people in your office who get on your nerves every day or who frighten you with their explosive tempers and sharp tongues?

Is your boss a cantankerous monster? Is your boss undependable, unreachable, or unpredictable? Does your boss play favorites? Is your boss a poor communicator or simply not the sharpest tool in the shed?

Do you ever feel as if you're trying to step lightly through a field of emotional land mines at work, but usually they explode in your face anyway?

If this describes your workplace, then sadly, you are not alone.

All Business Is Personal Perhaps the reason so many offices are unpleasant, inharmonious, dysfunctional places to work is that people fail to consider a basic fact: All business is personal.

Nonsense! you say. What about online stock transactions? What about all the deals that are sealed, contracts that are signed, and purchases that are completed without parties ever having to speak to each other, much less meeting face-to-face?

All these examples are personal because they involve human interaction and emotions such as fear, pride, and satisfaction. In fact, I defy you to come up with one example of business that does not—somehow—involve emotion. There's no escaping it. Even though something may come in a business wrapper, everything ultimately involves thoughts and feelings.

If you agree that thoughts and feelings are personal—that they are the very *definition* of all that is personal—you must also agree that you cannot designate the part of your life that is devoted to work or business as "impersonal."

Furthermore, work and business involve *interaction* with other people, which always has a personal element. Even if you're in business for yourself and working alone all day, you depend on *relationships* with your clients (and possibly suppliers). You are bound to have feelings about the people you interact with and about how you think they perceive you.

However, unless you are paying close attention, you may not always be entirely aware of what you are feeling. Becoming *self-aware* is an essential skill that you have to practice and develop over time.

The Emotional Animal in the Office

In most books about business skill and office savvy, emotion is a neglected topic. Why is this?

There are some antiquated stereotypes that still affect our thinking. Emotion is sloppy. Business is brisk and neat. Emotion is unpredictable and uncontrollable. Good business is the art of making everything manageable and keeping everything under control. Emotions must be reined in, or they'll get in the way of business.

But any workplace or office is a veritable bathhouse of cascading emotions and feelings, sloshing all over everyone. It always has been this way, and it always will be. So long as we are creatures of flesh and blood, not silicon and electronic circuitry, it can be no other way. Emotions may not be tangible, but trying to set them aside is patently unrealistic and therefore not very businesslike. In fact, most workers are just as motivated by emotional factors—self-respect, a sense of camaraderie, or a belief in their company's mission—as they are by the prospect of making more money.

Emotion does not only come with office romances or feuds. Emotions are screaming and singing all over the workplace every second. Just tune in and pay attention. If you keep your eyes and ears open, you'll see it and hear it, and you'll feel as if you have just woken from a dream.

But seeing and hearing is just the first part. What do you *do* with your awareness of emotion in the workplace? How do you put it to use?

Begin by understanding that emotions are good; they are your friends. Even the more difficult emotions like frustration and fear exist to tell us something, to prompt us to make necessary adjustments. When you see these "problematic" emotions arising in your coworkers, you may be in a position to help ease them through, to show them by word or deed that they are not alone, and that they need not suffer in silence. Ultimately, emotional intelligence creates a more efficient and effective workplace.

The Real "Bottom Line" This book is designed to help you keep your workplace relationships smooth and pleasant and to help you deal with common types of dysfunctional behavior in the office. Emotion is at the root of all this. As the Business Shrink, I get call after call from people fed up with their office life, and I can always trace the problems back to raw emotions.

You will learn how to combine emotional awareness and intelligence with the tools of logic and strategy to achieve your goals and to help you *feel better* in the workplace.

I will show you how to deal with the office bullies and raging incompetents who make you look bad or make you wish you were someplace else. By the time we are done, you are going to have a collection of tools that will help you deal with these pressures and lead a saner, healthful life *at work*. You will also enjoy an enhanced sense of self-respect and a better understanding of the emotional playing field of the workplace, along with the emerging rules for competing in it while keeping your dignity and sanity intact.

How you *feel* really matters. It matters a lot.

Before the material in this book can be effective, you must learn to recognize your feelings. That way, you can choose whether to let your feelings show or to edit how you express them. You can use this awareness and control, for example, to deliver a potentially tough message in a calm inviting manner. You can use it to recognize when the time has come to take a break or to nurture yourself in some fashion. You can use it to show appreciation or to express disapproval as well as to give advice most effectively. You can avoid blame and resentment. You can be more sensitive to others' needs, which is in your best interests as well as theirs. None of this comes automatically. It all takes practice, patience, and effort.

Fact and Fiction about Emotions and the Workplace

FICTION: Business is impersonal, and emotion has nothing to do with it.
FACT: All business is personal.

FICTION: You have to suppress emotion to do good business.
FACT: You need to be aware of your emotions—and other people's—to do good business and function well in the workplace.

FICTION: Knowing what you feel is easy and automatic.
FACT: It takes careful, deliberate attention to be aware of your own emotions and feelings. It also takes effort to

notice what other people may be feeling (judging by the clues they give).

FICTION: Emotions are a regrettable but unavoidable obstacle to getting work done efficiently.
FACT: Emotions provide the essential energy and motivation for getting anything done, and even so-called negative emotions like fear and anger have a useful purpose.

FICTION: The thing that mainly motivates a worker is the possibility of a raise.
FACT: Emotional factors—collaboration, cooperation, pride in a work product, and teamwork—motivate workers as much or more than money does.

1 the need for a humane and meaningful workplace

Do You Like Your Job? I don't care if you sweep floors, program computers, or run your own business and hire *other* people to sweep your floors and program your computers. I would bet that the way you feel about your job and the people you work with is one of the most powerful forces in your life. I bet it occupies your thoughts even when you're not working. I bet it colors the horizon of your days, even when you're on vacation. *Do you like your job?*

The answer to that question is likely to be the same as your answer to this question: *Do you like your workplace?*

Quiz: The Good, the Bad, and the Barely Tolerable Work Environment Try to answer as honestly and thoroughly as you can:

1. Do you like the company you work for? Are you proud to work there? Are you happy to be part of this organization?
2. Do you feel well treated at your job?
3. Do you feel appreciated for the work you do?
4. Do you like and respect your supervisor(s)?
5. Do you like and respect your employees?
6. Do you like and respect your coworkers?
7. Do you feel a sense of dread when you think about going to work?
8. How many times a day do you normally glance at the clock and mentally calculate how many hours remain until you can go home?

9. Are you excited about your future in this job?
10. Do you feel as if you have any control over how things get done?
11. Are your work relationships nurturing?
12. Are your work relationships unpleasant?

Scoring the Test

If this were one of those trendy self-help, find-your-dream-job-and-soul-mate-this-instant! books, you'd see some kind of point scale here.

Score one for each person you look forward to seeing at work. Subtract one point for each time you check the clock during a day at work. Now add up your score.

Twelve points or more: Your job is your nirvana. Eleven points: Nice catch! Eight to ten points: You got nothing to complain about. Four to seven points: Could be worse. One to three points: Sheer misery. Sorry.

Nope, this isn't that kind of quiz. I don't think it's useful to boil down your experience of your workplace in a formulaic way. Work is too complex for that. It's a world, a universe—and a universe has a lot of different stuff in it. But what this quiz *can* do is provide you with the opportunity to evaluate how satisfied you are with your working environment.

Why an Unhappy or Meaningless Workplace Is a Big Problem

In a February 2007 report, the Conference Board reported that Americans are increasingly unhappy with their jobs. Less than half of all Americans are satisfied with their jobs, down from 61 percent only twenty years ago. And this decline in job satisfaction—while highest among the newest entrants to the workforce, those under the age of twenty-five—is rampant among all workers no matter what their age, race, income, and place of residence.

These are alarming statistics. When people aren't happy, they do a crummy job. And when people feel like cogs in a wheel, they're not happy. This is the problem with many workplaces, perhaps even most.

Uninspired Workers = Unhappy Workers = Unproductive Workers

Peter Senge, in *The Fifth Discipline*, puts it this way: "When asked what they do for a living, most people describe the tasks they perform every day, not the *purpose* of the greater enterprise in which they take part. Most see themselves within a 'system' over which they have little or no influence. They 'do their job,' put in their time, and try to cope with forces outside of their control. Consequently, they tend to see their responsibilities as limited to the boundaries of their position. . . . When people in organizations focus only on their position, they have little sense of responsibility for the results produced when all positions interact. Moreover, when results are disappointing, it can be very difficult to know why. All you can do is to assume that 'someone screwed up.'"

In other words, in an uninspired organization, in an organization with no team vision, things don't get done right, and people don't care. Employees call in sick more often. They quit more often. And the bottom line suffers.

An unhappy worker is not going to put in the effort that a satisfied worker will. An unhappy worker doesn't care about the company's success. He just cares about his own misery, and as long as he's miserable, he'll want other people to be miserable, too. Misery loves company, as they say. Worker dissatisfaction can be contagious, spreading like rot throughout an organization.

Workers need to feel some sense of inspiration or at least satisfaction in their work. Otherwise, they have little incentive to be productive, other than the fear of losing a paycheck—and that only goes so far. But with satisfaction or inspiration, they find that not only are they productive, but they can inspire others as well.

The High Costs of Employee Turnover

Unhappy employees are a lot more likely to quit. As a general rule, it's a lot more expensive for companies to lose employees than it is to give raises. According to F. Leigh Branham, author of *Keeping the People Who Keep You in Business*, "The cost of hiring and training a new

Shallow Coworkers?
Or a Bigger Problem?

C Say I get a call from Dennis, who says, "There's a lot that's right about my job. I feel challenged, but not overworked. I feel well compensated. But I just *dread* coming in to work every day."

ME: Do you get along okay with your boss and coworkers?

DENNIS: Oh yeah. They're fine. They're good people. They're just not *my* kind of people.

ME: Well, what do you mean by that, Dennis? Do they vote Republican, and you vote Democrat?

DENNIS: Oh, I don't know how they vote. I don't even care. It's just like a different culture there. Maybe it's because they all have families and kids, and I'm a single guy. So we don't have the same interests necessarily.

ME: Hmmm . . . well, Dennis, that doesn't sound like an impossible situation to me. Many single guys get along real well with people who have families. You must have some common ground. Are you sure there isn't anything else that's bugging you?

DENNIS: Well, now that you mention it . . . sometimes I just feel like the people in my office are kind of shallow.

ME: Shallow? That's harsh language, Dennis. It sounds to me like you don't respect your workmates.

DENNIS: Well, I'm not disrespectful, but . . .

ME: I'm not saying you're wrong, Dennis. But from what you just said, you don't respect your workmates. But it would be interesting to know why. I mean, I understand why you'd hate going to work if you didn't respect your coworkers. That much I get. What you need to do, my friend, is figure out what exactly this *shallowness* is. So just watch and listen more closely for the next week or so, then get back to me.

• • •

The key to a situation like this is to find out what's *really* going on. Something was bugging Dennis, but it sounds to me as if there's more to the problem than his perception that his coworkers are shallow.

Sometimes, you don't even *know* why you hate your office. When that happens, it's important to figure out the real reason going into the office gives you a sinking feeling in your stomach. After all, you can't address the problem until you know what it is.

FOLLOW-UP: A WEEK LATER

DENNIS: Hey, Peter, you know what? The people in my office—they're not really shallow. That was a misjudgment on my part.

ME: Oh really? Well, I'm glad to hear that, Dennis. So are you starting to like them better now?

DENNIS: No, worse. They're not shallow; they're mean.

ME: Mean? Now that's an even stronger negative word! Can you give me an example?

DENNIS: Actually, they're mean, *and* they're a little shallow, too, and I can give you dozens of examples! Basically, all they do is talk about each other. They talk behind each other's backs. They kind of make it sound as if they're just kidding around or being ironically affectionate or something, but really they're always running down the guy who isn't in the room. Talking about his clothes, or her hair, or the way he fumbled that report, or the way she thinks she's going to get promoted but, *tsk tsk,* it's not likely. Sort of like that.

ME: So like, mean gossip?

DENNIS: Not exactly gossip, just a kind of mean-spirited banter that goes on all the time. And I never know what they say about me when I walk out of the room!

ME: Well, that does sound like a toxic work environment, Dennis. I wish I could give you a magic bullet to fix it, but it's not easy to change an entire office culture all by yourself.

DENNIS: It's like nobody has any sense of meaning or purpose about what they do, so they just run each other down.

ME: Well, a lack of meaning or mission can be a problem, too. But you don't have to participate in the obnoxious mean-spirited talk. You can keep your head above all that.

DENNIS: Yeah, I figure that's all I can do for the time being—maybe until I find another job!

ME: And while you're still at your current job, you can try to make the best of it. You could say to your coworkers, "Hey, it doesn't feel good to talk that way about so-and-so. That feels a little mean." Then change the subject to something positive. Or you can leave the room when the backbiting starts. If there is someone, anyone at work whom you trust and respect, ask that person what *he* thinks about all the mean talk. Maybe you can begin to form a kind of united front. Have a mini counterculture in your office. ∎

employee can vary greatly—from only a few thousand dollars for hourly employees to between $75,000 and $100,000 for top executives. Estimates of turnover costs range from 25 percent to almost 200 percent of annual compensation. Costs that are more difficult to estimate include customer service disruption, emotional costs, loss of morale, burnout/absenteeism among remaining employees, loss of experience, continuity, and 'corporate memory.'"

Whether it's from the inside looking out or the outside looking in, you can see this for yourself. Have you ever been a regular customer at a bank or a supermarket or a restaurant where the personnel is always changing? How does it make you feel? It's unsettling, right? Isn't it a lot more reassuring for customers to see the same faces instead of constantly seeing new ones? Did it ever make you change your favorite restaurant or your bank? Continuity is comforting. People like what's familiar.

From the inside, it's even more obvious how high turnover deflates morale. When you work with people day in and day out, you form some bonds with them and rely on them emotionally in subtle ways. When the people around you seem to change as often as you change your underwear, it makes you less secure and much less comfortable. It makes you wonder what the heck *you're* doing sticking around.

Apathy and Lack of Initiative

Apathy and lack of initiative can kill a company. Apathy means "I don't care," as in "I don't care about this job. I don't care about this company. I don't care about our customers." Lack of initiative means "I am passive about my work." In other words, "I am not here to offer my ideas or my spirit to this job. I reserve my creativity and passion for life—such as I have—for my off-hours."

Perhaps you can relate?

Managers and business owners had best take notice. No organization can survive long without caring, effort, and energy from its workers. Oddly enough, many companies fail to understand this.

In their book, *Values-Driven Business*, Ben Cohen and Mal Warwick explain, "What employees want and need the most is to be treated with dignity and respect as intelligent human beings capable of making their own contributions to the success of the company."

That doesn't sound like too much to ask, does it? So why do so few companies seem to offer this, especially since it is in their own best interests to do so?

From Units to Humans: A Brief History

Many problems and dysfunctional attitudes found in the workplace date back to the abuses of early American capitalism. Classical economists and social scientists used to look at workers as either a huge glob of folks ("labor") or as individual units (not humans, *units*) whose productivity could be increased by applying a scientific formula (sort of like finding new ways to make the same donkey carry more weight while rewarding it with the same amount of hay). You're probably familiar with the high-powered entrepreneurs known as robber barons who built the railroads and dug the coal mines of nineteenth-century America on the bleeding backs of immigrants.

Robber barons were not exactly from the touchy-feely school of management. Their astonishing abuses—such as inhumane working hours and conditions, brutal supervisors, and meager wages—led to the formation of labor unions. Some of the most successful, historically important unions were in Detroit. After years of lockouts and strikes, during the 1930s and 1940s, the members of the United Auto Workers union enjoyed the highest earnings, benefits, and overall quality of life for industrial workers anywhere in the world. The UAW also admitted African Americans while other unions continued to shut them out. Because of the UAW, children of assembly line workers went to college alongside sons and daughters of bankers and lawyers, earning the credentials that provided them with the keys to the American corridors of power.

The automobile industry did not go willingly into an era of enlightened and humane treatment for its workers. Rather, it was bludgeoned into its progressive personnel policies by the disciplined membership of the UAW.

The reason for Detroit's current decline in the face of foreign competition is complex, but those who blame workers' benefits for the slump are simply wrong. In fact, foreign car companies have learned from the exemplary policies and practices of our domestic automotive factories.

Unions Pave the Way

Unions are, in essence, a collective and institutional response to the many problems created by abusive management. There is strength in numbers, and the middle class owes its evolution, in large part, to the unions. Without unions, most owners would have kept workers at survival wages. Your weekends and eight-hour days (as opposed to twelve-hour days seven days a week), paid overtime, holidays, and employer-paid health benefits are a direct result of industrial-age unions and the terrible risks their members took, and the people they lost to violence. Europe's unions won even greater concessions, and their agendas led to comprehensive national health care in much of the modern world. The list of benefits achieved as a direct result of unions goes on.

Even The World Bank—not exactly a pro-labor entity—published a report in 2002 arguing that unions are generally good for economies because they raise everybody's standard of living. Higher pay means workers have more money to spend, which is good for every sector.

An Early Business Visionary: Sidney Harman

One of America's great business leaders, Dr. Sidney Harman, executive chairman of Harman International, pioneered the high-fidelity audio industry right after World War II.

When young Army Intelligence captain Sidney Harman returned to the United States after the war, he began visiting different organizations in hopes of learning how to build and maintain a successful company. He was shocked to discover that businesses often treated workers with contempt and denied them their dignity.

Dr. Harman chose the opposite path, treating workers as partners and creating a highly enjoyable and responsive work environment, a place that workers were proud to call their own. Like his business, Harman's employees thrived.

Harman fostered such a positive and respectful environment that once people went to work for a Harman brand, they rarely left. Even today, when Harman International employees invent an improvement to a product, they are richly rewarded and celebrated. Bosses such as Harman understand the symbiotic relationship between labor and management.

The Shrinks and Sociologists Weigh In

Harman's approach was unusual at the time he launched his business. But as early as the 1930s, researchers had begun to view the workplace not only as an economic system, but also as a new kind of social system with a life of its own affected by group norms and personal interactions between managers and employees. Psychologists and behavioral scientists rushed in where once only economists had dared to tread. This changed everything. A century and a half into the Industrial Age, industrial and organizational entities have combined to become places of people as well as of money.

MIT Sloan School of Management professor Doug McGregor was one of the most influential social philosophers of the twentieth century. His book *The Human Side of Enterprise* (1960) is one of the great landmarks in organizational theory, and its observations and conclusions, albeit in greatly modified and annotated form, exert considerable influence to this day.

McGregor proposed what he dubbed the Theory X and Theory Y of human behavior. It was a breakthrough in the study of workplace motivation. Theory X, which describes the predominant management attitude of the fifties, argues that workers are lazy and unmotivated. They hate to work and would rather avoid responsibility. According to Theory X, workers need narrowly defined tasks, with close and constant supervision, plus base incentives like money and job security to encourage productivity.

Theory Y, which McGregor subscribed to, proposes that workers are creative, ambitious, and self-motivated. Ultimately, they crave responsibility and will perform at an optimum level without much supervision.

McGregor argued that a manager's belief in Theory X or Y would influence his managerial style. In fact, management styles began to change in the 1960s, in large part as a result of the book.

Two Philosophies of Management   More than offering an analysis of workers, McGregor was proposing a philosophy of management. He stated that if a manager believes his employees are like either X or Y, then he should manage them accordingly. However, McGregor believed Theory Y offered a better description of reality, and he convinced enough people to revolutionize contemporary methods of supervision and management.

The fluid and expanding nature of today's global economy—based on information rather than on fixed tasks and job descriptions—means that companies and managers lacking the vision to take a Theory Y approach risk being left in the twentieth century. Creativity, adaptability, and initiative are worker qualities that become increasingly necessary as the worlds of commerce and technology continue to accelerate and change form.

The value of the individual worker is recognized today more than ever, and that's good for business and for you.

But it's not quite nirvana yet in our American work force, as you know. Nearly fifty years have passed since

the
ters

nie, a bank teller, who compares his job to counting
e says, "That's all I do and it's all any of the tellers do.
y. We count it out so that our customers can see: 'Twenty,
hundred, a hundred and twenty. There you go and have

it than that," argues his friend and fellow teller, Joe.
cords, we have to enter data, we have to fill out forms."
nnie, unenthusiastically.
el your job is meaningless," says Joe. "But I think it's a

Bennie. "And you know what? There are a lot of neces-
achines do, too. Some day, they'll get robots to do our
matter of a few simple algorithms. I mean, face it, Joe. The
wall the day they invented the ATM."
kes to work around Bennie. Not that he's unpleasant, but
opinion of his job that he makes the other tellers feel
jobs as well, even though they try not to be affected by
stomers pick up on his attitude. Though no one has com-
nie, he makes the bank a less welcoming place.
e goes out to lunch with Joe and another teller, Linda.
ie," says Linda. "There are worse jobs out there than ours."
e that," says Bennie.
"I have a cousin who's in *jail*. He makes license plates for
alk about *meaningless*!"
points out Bennie dryly.
ut those kids who make sneakers in sweat shops in devel-
demands Linda. "Now *that's* a lousy job!"
his trademark world-weary sigh. "You guys," he says,
or trying to cheer me up. I'm glad you're glad to work at
e job. And it's stupid. It's automatic. It's empty. Yes, there
nd there are *immoral* jobs. I'm glad we're not working in
But look, leave me to my misery, okay? I'm not satisfied
nd, meaningless job, with no creativity, and no greater pur-
ng beans."
have your misery," retorts Linda.
d-end job though," protests Joe. "You could become a loan
ortant. You can help people get loans to buy their first house."

McGregor published his book, but a lot—probably most—
of corporate and business leaders still don't quite get it.

Back to You

So what do you do if, after all is said and done, your boss
is no Sidney Harman? What if the president of your company has never heard of Doug McGregor, much less read
his book? What do you do if you don't belong to a union,
or if your union has won you a decent wage but can't
protect you from the ravages of disrespect, meaninglessness,
inconsiderate bosses, and petty, untrustworthy coworkers?

You are at a crossroads in history, my friend. The world
is ready for a new kind of employee, one who takes control of her life at work and who insists on respect and
civility all around. You have resources today that workers never had, never even dreamed of, fifty or sixty years
ago. There are grievance procedures, nondiscrimination
statutes, laws against harassment. Theoretically, at least,
you can protect yourself against your boss or coworker
if one of them mistreats you. In addressing the problems
of a dysfunctional work environment, it is important
to understand the legal and procedural devices at your
command.

But you have twenty-first-century emotional resources
as well—wisdom resources, if you will. That's what we're
here to talk about, most of all, in this book. Where is your
emotional point of leverage in any work environment?
What kind of personal power do you have to affect your
workplace?

And most of all—what do you want out of your day-
to-day experience at work?

Or, what is it that you *don't* want but that you've had
to put up with for some time?

McWorkers

Regardless of your age or professional level, you may be
at a point when you don't get to call the shots. Whether

you are eighteen or fifty-eight, nothing sucks the joy out of life faster than working at a job you despise.

Maybe you have an abusive boss, or your coworkers are bullies and whiners who badmouth each other and try to steal one another's good ideas. Maybe your job affords no growth opportunities or is simply the wrong fit for you. Or maybe—dare I even mention it—you're working a *McJob*.

A McJob has come to mean the lowest and most insipid of employment niches. Though the term refers to the McDonald's hamburger chain, it has a much wider application. The common denominator is that a McJob is repetitive, dull, unchallenging, disrespected, and poorly paid. Even if you are not working a stereotypically menial service-sector job, a mundane office job that lacks any sort of meaning beyond a paycheck could be considered a white-collar McJob, which is just about as bad.

Just because a job isn't glamorous or well paid doesn't mean it has to be a McJob. We need workers to provide basic services to society. We desperately need people to punch the tickets, mop the floors, clean the bathrooms, and serve the food. All the same, too often such jobs fail to evoke a glowing sense of pride. Such jobs are honor-

---

❝ ❞ Advice for managers: The buck stops with you.

As a manager, you set the tone for the office. As Harry Truman tried to teach all executives, the buck stops with you. According to *Management Issues News,* "The 2005 Workplace Productivity Survey conducted by the Society for Human Resource Management (SHRM) found that almost six out of ten (58 percent) Americans identified poor management as the biggest obstacle to productivity." (*http://www.shrm.org/press_published/CMS_011140.asp*)

It is up to you to maintain a positive, motivated workplace and to establish open lines of communication to sustain such an environment. You must be sensitive to emotional undercurrents in the office, and alert to your team members' needs and vulnerabilities.

---

able, yes, certainly. An
mate purpose is hon
Rewarding? Not for

So what do you d
cousin of a McJob, or
older relative of a Mc

Even though it m
have options.

We live in a mobil
ety. Your current job
life, a temporary mear
you are young. Millior
put in their time back
tables, bagging groceri
floors. In the best of
majority of service jo
ple who are just gettir
world of gainful empl
with the mundane ch
getting paid for it.

Make a Plan   Whether you have
ply unfulfilling, you ha
working your way thro
research within your
there is any room for
position. Whatever yo
the end of the road. I
unknowable railroad of

Just for a moment,
suggest that you can fi
any job, so long as it
criminal or harmful to
your duties conscientio
to take permanent satisf
can be some satisfacti
worth looking for, ackn

CASE ST

**Bennie ar
Bean Cou**

Visualize
beans. B
We count out m
forty, sixty, eight
a nice weekend.
"There's mor
"We have to kee
"Woo-hoo," says
"I'm sorry yo
necessary servic
"Sure it is," s
sary services tha
job. It should be
writing was on
No one muc
he has such a lo
demeaned by th
him. Worse, the
plained about B
One day Ben
"I tell you, B
"I won't disp
Joe chimes i
pennies an hou
"It's a servic
"And what a
oping countries
Bennie give
"thanks so muc
the bank. It's a
are worse jobs.
those industries
working a dead
pose than coun
"Fine, you c
"It's not a d
officer. That's im

McGregor published his book, but a lot—probably most—of corporate and business leaders still don't quite get it.

Back to You   So what do you do if, after all is said and done, your boss is no Sidney Harman? What if the president of your company has never heard of Doug McGregor, much less read his book? What do you do if you don't belong to a union, or if your union has won you a decent wage but can't protect you from the ravages of disrespect, meaninglessness, inconsiderate bosses, and petty, untrustworthy coworkers?

You are at a crossroads in history, my friend. The world is ready for a new kind of employee, one who takes control of her life at work and who insists on respect and civility all around. You have resources today that workers never had, never even dreamed of, fifty or sixty years ago. There are grievance procedures, nondiscrimination statutes, laws against harassment. Theoretically, at least, you can protect yourself against your boss or coworker if one of them mistreats you. In addressing the problems of a dysfunctional work environment, it is important to understand the legal and procedural devices at your command.

But you have twenty-first-century emotional resources as well—wisdom resources, if you will. That's what we're here to talk about, most of all, in this book. Where is your emotional point of leverage in any work environment? What kind of personal power do you have to affect your workplace?

And most of all—what do you want out of your day-to-day experience at work?

Or, what is it that you *don't* want but that you've had to put up with for some time?

McWorkers

Regardless of your age or professional level, you may be at a point when you don't get to call the shots. Whether you are eighteen or fifty-eight, nothing sucks the joy out of life faster than working at a job you despise.

Maybe you have an abusive boss, or your coworkers are bullies and whiners who badmouth each other and try to steal one another's good ideas. Maybe your job affords no growth opportunities or is simply the wrong fit for you. Or maybe—dare I even mention it—you're working a *McJob*.

A McJob has come to mean the lowest and most insipid of employment niches. Though the term refers to the McDonald's hamburger chain, it has a much wider application. The common denominator is that a McJob is repetitive, dull, unchallenging, disrespected, and poorly paid. Even if you are not working a stereotypically menial service-sector job, a mundane office job that lacks any sort of meaning beyond a paycheck could be considered a white-collar McJob, which is just about as bad.

Just because a job isn't glamorous or well paid doesn't mean it has to be a McJob. We need workers to provide basic services to society. We desperately need people to punch the tickets, mop the floors, clean the bathrooms, and serve the food. All the same, too often such jobs fail to evoke a glowing sense of pride. Such jobs are honor-

66 99 | Advice for managers: The buck stops with you.

As a manager, you set the tone for the office. As Harry Truman tried to teach all executives, the buck stops with you. According to *Management Issues News,* "The 2005 Workplace Productivity Survey conducted by the Society for Human Resource Management (SHRM) found that almost six out of ten (58 percent) Americans identified poor management as the biggest obstacle to productivity." (*http://www.shrm.org/press_published/CMS_011140.asp*)

It is up to you to maintain a positive, motivated workplace and to establish open lines of communication to sustain such an environment. You must be sensitive to emotional undercurrents in the office, and alert to your team members' needs and vulnerabilities.

able, yes, certainly. Any honest work that serves a legitimate purpose is honorable and dignified. But fulfilling? Rewarding? Not for most of us.

So what do you do if you are stuck in a McJob, the cousin of a McJob, or a softer, genteel, more comfortable older relative of a McJob?

Even though it may not always feel like it, you do have options.

We live in a mobile, fast-paced, rapidly changing society. Your current job may be just a placeholder in your life, a temporary means of paying the bills, particularly if you are young. Millions of successful career professionals put in their time back in their teens and twenties waiting tables, bagging groceries, pumping gasoline, and sweeping floors. In the best of all worlds, in my opinion, the vast majority of service jobs would be filled by young people who are just getting their feet wet in the wonderful world of gainful employment. Think of it as helping out with the mundane chores like laundry or garbage—but getting paid for it.

Make a Plan   Whether you have a McJob or a position that is simply unfulfilling, you have to have a plan. You can begin working your way through college or night school or do research within your company and determine whether there is any room for advancement to a more fulfilling position. Whatever you do, remember that this job isn't the end of the road. It's a way station on the vast and unknowable railroad of your life.

Just for a moment, I want to go out on a limb and suggest that you can find some meaning in pretty much any job, so long as it is decent, honest work (i.e., not criminal or harmful to anyone) and you're performing your duties conscientiously. This doesn't mean you have to take permanent satisfaction in that job, only that there can be some satisfaction available. That satisfaction is worth looking for, acknowledging, and cultivating.

Bennie and the Bean Counters

Visualize Bennie, a bank teller, who compares his job to counting beans. Bennie says, "That's all I do and it's all any of the tellers do. We count out money. We count it out so that our customers can see: 'Twenty, forty, sixty, eighty, a hundred, a hundred and twenty. There you go and have a nice weekend.'"

"There's more to it than that," argues his friend and fellow teller, Joe. "We have to keep records, we have to enter data, we have to fill out forms."

"Woo-hoo," says Bennie, unenthusiastically.

"I'm sorry you feel your job is meaningless," says Joe. "But I think it's a necessary service."

"Sure it is," says Bennie. "And you know what? There are a lot of necessary services that machines do, too. Some day, they'll get robots to do our job. It should be a matter of a few simple algorithms. I mean, face it, Joe. The writing was on the wall the day they invented the ATM."

No one much likes to work around Bennie. Not that he's unpleasant, but he has such a low opinion of his job that he makes the other tellers feel demeaned by their jobs as well, even though they try not to be affected by him. Worse, the customers pick up on his attitude. Though no one has complained about Bennie, he makes the bank a less welcoming place.

One day Bennie goes out to lunch with Joe and another teller, Linda.

"I tell you, Bennie," says Linda. "There are worse jobs out there than ours."

"I won't dispute that," says Bennie.

Joe chimes in. "I have a cousin who's in *jail*. He makes license plates for *pennies an hour*. Talk about *meaningless*!"

"It's a service," points out Bennie dryly.

"And what about those kids who make sneakers in sweat shops in developing countries?" demands Linda. "Now *that's* a lousy job!"

Bennie gives his trademark world-weary sigh. "You guys," he says, "thanks so much for trying to cheer me up. I'm glad you're glad to work at the bank. It's a fine job. And it's stupid. It's automatic. It's empty. Yes, there are worse jobs. And there are *immoral* jobs. I'm glad we're not working in those industries. But look, leave me to my misery, okay? I'm not satisfied working a dead-end, meaningless job, with no creativity, and no greater purpose than counting beans."

"Fine, you can have your misery," retorts Linda.

"It's not a dead-end job though," protests Joe. "You could become a loan officer. That's important. You can help people get loans to buy their first house."

"Mmm," says Bennie. "Thanks for pointing that out, Joe. I think I'll pass."

Remarkably, the following week, Joe and Linda are willing to invite Bennie out with them for lunch again. They're either gluttons for punishment or saints. But this week, Linda's got news: a new boyfriend!

"And I met him at work!" she announces triumphantly to Bennie. "He came to my window. He's been coming for a long time, and he always comes up to my window, and that's how I knew something was up."

"Well, that's meaningful for you," acknowledges Bennie. "Congratulations."

"See, there is a human element to being a teller," remarks Joe.

Bennie guffaws. He's already married. He doesn't need to meet women at the bank. But a thought occurs to him. "I don't know why, but I've never even had a customer so much as smile at me or ask how I was. And here, you've got a guy coming in and flirting. No wonder you like your job."

Joe says, "Well, that's funny. Customers are nice to me all the time. There's a bunch of them I'm friendly with, I know, and I enjoy seeing. Sometimes I get a little gift, a little holiday card or something. Don't you have any favorite customers, Bennie? Or do you scorn the whole notion of customer service? Is the very idea of it beneath you?"

"What customer service?" asks Bennie. "They just want me to count their beans. And I do. Every day."

Linda laughs. "*Lighten up already*, Bennie."

At lunch the following week, Bennie makes a confession. "I don't exactly love my job now, but I had a pretty good week. I started noticing people, and saying hello and how are you, and really listening. I guess any contact with people has some meaning, if you're really there for it, and paying attention."

"Wow," says Linda. "So you've had a change of heart then? You don't just feel like a bean counter anymore?"

"Not entirely," admits Bennie. "I was inspired by your story last week, Linda. You can have a genuine exchange with people, even if it's just a few moments or minutes. It makes the job a little less dreary."

"Uh-oh," says Joe. "I better warn Bennie's wife."

Of course, not only Bennie benefited from his reformed attitude; his coworkers, the customers who came to his window, and the bank benefited as well. Bennie no longer scared people away with his cynicism. ■

When you show up every day, do your work well, and soldier on for the betterment of yourself and your family, you can be proud of your tenacity and strength. Many people can't hack this; they choose unemployment and end up either on the streets or scavenging from relatives and friends. I think a good janitor demonstrates more dignity than a parasitic househusband with a never-ending novel in the works. I'm not suggesting you should abandon working on your novel or dreaming of a more colorful life, but I *am* saying that you have control over how you think and can choose from any number of proactive measures.

Consider dishwashing, not the most prestigious of occupations. We all do the dishes at home, though, don't we? Is it so bad? Thich Nhat Hanh is a world-famous Vietnamese monk whom Dr. Martin Luther King Jr. nominated for the Nobel Peace Prize in 1967. Here is what he has to say about washing dishes:

To my mind, the idea that doing the dishes is unpleasant can occur only when you are not doing them. Once you are standing in front of the sink with your sleeves rolled up and your hands in warm water, it really is not so bad. I enjoy taking my time with each dish, being fully aware of the dish, the water, and each movement of my hands. I know that if I hurry in order to go and have a cup of tea, the time will be unpleasant and not worth living. That would be a pity, for each minute, each second of life is a miracle. . . . Washing the dishes is at the same time a means and an end. That is, not only do we do the dishes in order to have clean dishes, we also do the dishes just to do the dishes, to live fully in each moment while washing them. (*A Lifetime of Peace: Essential Writings by and About Thich Nhat Hanh*, ed. Jennifer Schwamm Willis. Marlowe & Co.: 2003)

That's a pretty enlightened attitude. Maybe we're not all ready to appreciate the miracle of every second (though there's no reason why we shouldn't, if we want to), but we can start with a positive appreciation of what we have.

You Work for Yourself

A job is ephemeral and transitory. You can think of any particular job as a chapter in the book of your life, rather than the entire story. This will make it easier to deal with a job that is not necessarily your dream job, and it will also help recast almost any job into a satisfying experience (at least temporarily). No matter what, the one thing you can always change—the one thing that you have the most control over on the job—is you.

Whether you are the only employee of a sole proprietorship or one of a thousand secretaries in a multinational corporation, you ultimately work for yourself. Of course you must work toward your company's goals and within certain parameters, but you are simultaneously working to achieve personal aims as well.

If you don't like your job, don't respect your boss, and couldn't give a hoot about your company's mission, you should consider quitting and going to work for someone else at a new job. That's one of the blessings of our capitalist society; you have that choice.

Why Meaning Matters

There are many factors that can make you feel better about your work. In recent years, researchers have found that job satisfaction and pride in one's work are also linked to the employer's contributions to the community—contributions not directly tied to the profit motive. This makes sense, because whatever work you do, you also have a relationship with your community and the world—and so does your company. Your company has an internal relationship with its employees and an external one with the community. Often, these relationships are a reflection of each other.

Think of your relationships as concentric circles with you in the center, your close friends and family at the

next level, then your outer circle of friends, your coworkers, your community, your city, your country, and finally
the whole world.

Work is not separate from your relationship to the
rest of the world. Remember, *all business is personal.* What
could be more personal than the activity that you engage
in every day? Where you spend most of your waking
hours, what happens there, and what you do there to a
large degree define your sense of self and self-worth. In a
nutshell, that's why meaning matters.

Exit Quiz   So I'll ask you again: *How do you feel about your job? Why
are you in this job?* If you feel as if you've answered those
questions already, may I suggest that answering them
three, four, or five times is better. These are good questions to ask often—yearly, monthly, even weekly.

Think about the following questions with the same
degree of thoughtfulness, patience, and sincerity that you
brought to this chapter's opening quiz.

1. Are there people in your workplace who bring
   their personal problems to work in a way that dis-
   turbs you and disrupts your work? **》 CHAPTER 2**
2. Do any of your coworkers flat-out scare you with
   their meanness or nasty temper? **》 CHAPTER 2**
3. Is your working environment fraught with conflict or tension? **》 CHAPTER 3**
4. Do you feel that your boss is cruel, irresponsible,
   even a little nuts? **》 CHAPTER 4**
5. Do you have trouble dealing with your boss's
   moods? **》 CHAPTER 5**
6. How can you improve your relationship with
   your boss or supervisor? **》 CHAPTER 5**
7. Is there unstated "sexual politics"? **》 CHAPTER 6**
8. How can you improve relations with your coworkers? **》 CHAPTER 7**

9. What can you do to make life at the office easier, friendlier, and more efficient? **》 CHAPTERS 3, 7, AND THE CONCLUSION**

10. How can you improve your own attitude toward work, and make it better for yourself? **》 CONCLUSION**

Symptoms of a "Meaning-Deficient" Work Environment

- Workers often call in sick.
- There is a lack of passion—a sense of apathy about the workplace.
- Workers never express initiative or creativity.
- There is high turnover.
- Workers gossip a lot and backbite.
- Workers glance at the clock or at their watches a lot.
- Nobody knows—or cares—what people in other departments are doing.

2 dysfunctional personalities in the workplace

Chronically Difficult People

Certain personality types are simply difficult no matter how much you try to develop a smooth, amicable relationship with them. They are not just difficult in particular situations, rather because of an inherent aspect of their character—generally one completely beyond their control—they create problems in every circumstance.

It's best not to blame people for being who they are and doing what they do. Such people have bad mental habits and are usually unhappy. Understanding the types of difficult people will help you develop the diplomatic skills necessary to work with them on a daily basis.

The Passive-Aggressive Coworker

Passive-aggressive behavior is extremely common, not to mention annoying. Passive-aggressive people habitually embarrass, irritate, or inconvenience other people, and they do so in a way that looks innocent on the surface, even though it is not.

A passive-aggressive coworker's performance is likely to be slightly subpar, especially when others are depending on him. Not grossly deficient, mind you, but just deficient enough to make others sweat, look bad, or have to work a little harder than they would otherwise.

A passive-aggressive colleague will borrow your desk stapler and forget to return it. Passive-aggressive workers may take more sick days than other people, arrive a little late, and miss deadlines. They always have a good excuse, and you might feel like a monster for getting upset with them. But actually, as psychologists explain, the passive-aggressive is already angry at *you*. In fact, the passive-aggressive is angry in general. But because they are afraid to express anger directly, they deny and suppress it, so their repressed anger spills out all over the place in "passive" ways that bug the heck out of those around them.

If you get angry at a passive-aggressive, you're actually giving him what he secretly wants. (It's so secret, in fact, that he doesn't even admit to it—or perhaps even *realize* it—himself.) Because he is afraid to get angry, *your* expression of anger functions as a surrogate for his own, providing him with a kind of twisted, indirect release.

Handling the Passive-Aggressive Personality

It's unlikely you can help a passive-aggressive person "heal" unless he realizes that he has a problem (in which case he will, you hope, enlist the services of a competent therapist). However, there are ways of handling passive-aggressive coworkers that will save you a lot of grief.

When dealing with this sort of personality, always be very, very direct and concrete about your expectations. Don't give him wiggle room. A common passive-aggressive explanation for behavior is "Oh, I thought you said you wanted *this*, not *that*." Avoid this situation by communicating in ways that are unambiguous. Avoid metaphors and generalities. You may even want to write down your agreements to guard against this behavior. Try this tactfully by positioning this to the passive-aggressive coworker as a way of "reminding us both, in case we forget."

Never threaten a passive-aggressive person. Ooh, he loves that! Rather, set up clear, firm, reasonable consequences for his behavior, and make sure he knows what to expect from you. For example, if you are working on a project together, and the work you have to do on the project depends to some degree on the passive-aggressive completing *his* part in a timely fashion, inform him in advance that you'll be documenting, for purposes of good record-keeping, the times at which you both met the project's milestones. At the end of the project, make clear that the boss will have access to this documentation. But do not assume authority that you do not possess over a peer. Always make it clear that these same consequences will apply to you as well.

Frame the consequences you impose in terms of your own feelings (which are unquestionable), not in terms of a judgment about the passive-aggressive person. For example, let's say a passive-aggressive friend borrows money from you (before you realize she is passive-aggressive), then takes three or four times as long as promised to pay you back, prompting you to remind her every once in a while, and then to feel sickeningly guilty when she looks abashed and says, "Oh, of course, I'm so sorry! I just had a really bad week." You react by agonizing over whether you *really* need that $200. Finally, after you have paid a rather high price in stress and discomfort, she pays you

66 99   **Advice for managers:** Turn negativity around.

Gary Topchik is the author of *Managing Workplace Negativity* and the CEO of SilverStar Enterprises. His consulting firm has shown companies like Oracle, Dow Jones, and Disney how to transform employee attitudes in the workplace. Topchik says, "I like to treat negativity as a behavior problem." While visiting my radio show, he reminded me that some people come to work each day in a negative mood. They have what Topchik calls a negative personality, and they spread that negativity around. "They [troublesome workers] have to be told, 'When you say such-and-such, you're expressing negativity, or when you do this, or you get this expression on your face, you're spreading negativity throughout the office.'

"I also encourage managers to set a time limit for negativity. For example, you could say to an unhappy employee, 'Okay, for the first five minutes of our meeting, just tell me what's going wrong. But when 9:05 hits . . . we're going to talk solutions.'"

Topchik recommends counseling the negative person to vent his feelings—but not at the entire office. Tell the negative person to find a buddy in the workplace, someone he can discuss his concerns and frustrations with.

in dribs and drabs. The next time the passive-aggressive friend comes to you and says, "Listen, I know this is asking a lot, especially since I took so long to pay you back last time, but my sister is getting married next month, and my mom *really* wants to fly out for the wedding. None of us can afford to pay for her entire plane fare right now because she lives in rural Louisiana, and she actually has to make *three* connections plus the airport shuttle. She doesn't want to take a bus because of her arthritis, so I was just wondering if I could *at least ask* . . ." STOP! Hold up your hand in a "halt" gesture and say, "I'm sorry, but I can't lend you money anymore. It was really stressful for me last time when I had to remind you to pay me back. So I don't want to open myself up to that kind of stress again. Good luck with your mom." Note that your response focused on *your* feelings and not on the passive-aggressive person's feelings in the matter.

Keep everything rooted in the here and now. Refrain from compiling a list of grievances against the person. If you bring up past misbehavior that has no bearing on the present circumstance, chances are you'll get a cloying apology that will make you sick or make you feel like a heartless beast—or both. Do not imagine that the passive-aggressive personality is rational, even if she or he is intelligent and uses words well.

On the other hand, hold the passive-aggressive accountable in a dispassionate, straightforward way. Say, "You said you'd do this, and you did not." Or, "You said that, and it was not true, and you knew it. That is not okay." Just don't get angry. The passive-aggressive will be flabbergasted by your moral courage. Above all, limit your dealings with the person and set boundaries. For example:

> *"No, you may not work on my computer while I'm in the conference room. I have a lot of documents open, I have everything on my desk set up in a certain way, and I just don't feel comfortable having someone else working in my space."*

"Actually, I can't work with you on the next project. I am going to work with Joe Schmoe instead—he and I haven't worked together yet, and I think he has some great ideas."

"I'm afraid you can't have my stapler again. I'll need it."

He may react by trying to ingratiate himself with you, making an extra effort to engage you or greet you when you come to work, or even do something generous (though unsolicited) for you. All this can be confusing. Stand firm. Thank him when appropriate, but don't get sucked in. Passive-aggressive personalities do understand limits, sooner or later.

The Sniper Snipers are psychological cousins of passive-aggressive personalities. Snipers don't have the same range of annoying behaviors, but they strike often and without warning with subtle verbal digs, "humorous" disparaging remarks, insulting innuendoes, and derisive facial expressions. Like their cousins, they are largely unconscious of what they do and often afraid of their own hostility. Some of them are just trying to draw a little attention in a perverse way.

The best way to deal with a sniper is to call her on her sniping as it happens.

"Hey, Bill, that came out as mean. You didn't mean to hurt my feelings, did you?"

"Gosh, Claudia, why did you roll your eyes? Did what I just said seem silly to you?"

"Todd, I can't say I found that last remark funny. It sounded more nasty than funny."

You need a lot of self-awareness to catch snipers in the moment. Otherwise, you may not even realize that you have been sniped until minutes or even hours later,

Disarming a Sniper

LARRY: Hey, Peter, you know, there's this one guy at work I just can't stand. He doesn't just disagree or compete. He has no *limits* with the nasty things he'll say. He calls people names, he threatens, he puts people down. He does it to everyone but especially to me for some reason. I try to be reasonable, but he doesn't reason. I try not to let it get to me, but I can't help it.

ME: Well, how often do you have to interact with this guy?

LARRY: We work in the same office space, so I see him every day. I feel like punching him in the nose.

ME: Well, I wouldn't advise that, Larry. Let me ask you this. You say he bothers other people, too?

LARRY: Oh, yeah. But no one as much as me.

ME: How do other people handle him?

LARRY: They just . . . I don't know what they do!

ME: Well, for some reason, this guy picks on you more than anyone else. Does it have to do with the fact he works more closely with you than with anyone else?

LARRY: No. Our projects and assignments don't really overlap too often. He just *aims* his unpleasantness at me for some reason. At other people too, I guess, but not nearly as much.

ME: Hmm. Well, let me suggest something, Larry. You say he also gets on other

people's cases. Watch what they do. Watch how they handle him. They may have something figured out about this guy that you haven't yet.

• • •

Try not to get too angry at snipers, and don't take their sniping personally. It's unlikely that you are their only victim. Snipers tend to become unpopular pretty quickly in a work environment. There may be a few people, like the boss, whom they dare not snipe at, but a sniper always has multiple victims, and her game rapidly becomes obvious to everyone.

Treat the sniper civilly and with respect. Never snipe, swipe, or dig in turn. Don't lower yourself to the sniper's level; bring the conversation up a notch or two. Look the sniper in the eye and speak directly, with clarity and conviction. Be a role model; snipers are often not beyond redemption.

In this case, Larry's coworkers had clearly evolved a strategy for handling the sniper. It was important to find out what it was so Larry could use it as well.

FOLLOW-UP: A WEEK LATER

When Larry calls again, he tells me, "You know what I noticed, Peter? Most people actually *laugh* at the guy when he gets nasty! I mean, it's not that they laugh *in his face* exactly, but they all have this sort of repressed giggle when they respond to him."

ME: So they don't take him seriously.

LARRY: Apparently not.

ME: Maybe that's the difference between you and everybody else. He senses that they're laughing at him, and it diffuses him. He knows he can't get under their skin. If anything, they feel sorry for him.

LARRY: Well, I don't feel sorry for him. And I don't find him remotely funny.

ME: Well, maybe you could start by telling him a joke then, next time.

LARRY: Are you kidding? A joke?

ME: Sure. Next time he goes off on you, say, Hey, I got a good joke. Just do that for a while and see how it goes.

LARRY: What if I don't know any jokes?

ME: Look for some online. They don't have to be *good* jokes. In fact, maybe if they're bad jokes, it's all the better! Just change the energy with this guy, Larry. He isn't *dangerous*. He's not a threat. I can tell you that much, because if he were a scary guy, your coworkers wouldn't be laughing at him. ∎

and by then it's too late—all you can do is feel a little bruised and resentful or, even worse yet, stupid for having been stung when you weren't aware of it. That's what the sniper wants, albeit unconsciously.

The Nosy Coworker   As most of us know, people who can't mind their own business are a nuisance. There are always one or two busybodies in every office. You know the drill: "Hey there, what are you working on?" "I saw you and Darlene go out to lunch—are you guys dating or something?" "Hey, do you mind if I read your presentation? I'm just curious."

Nosy coworkers are harmless for the most part and even a bit funny. At times, it's easy to laugh them off. But sometimes these coworkers are also jealous or sneakily competitive and would love to undermine you if they could. You can usually sense which type of person you are dealing with. In any case, deal with this type of coworker by briskly setting forth your limits in no uncertain terms. Nosy people will understand if you say:

"Please don't poke your head into my office anymore unless it's about business."

"Please don't comment on my clothes anymore. It makes me feel uncomfortable."

"I'd prefer you don't ask me about my personal life. I'm a very private person."

The Know-It-All   Know-it-alls broadcast that they're the only ones who are really competent, the only ones who really understand the business, the only ones who are indispensable. In fact, no one else's judgment or ideas are worth the time of day. Know-it-alls are condescending and arrogant, but they can also be amusing when they're not bugging the heck out of you. The real danger is that they can be convincing. Especially if you're new to a particular workplace or the know-it-all is your supervisor, his or her airtight convictions can aggravate your self-doubt.

To counteract a know-it-all, be clear about your job and your objectives and know your own stuff. You don't need to impress the know-it-all, and you certainly don't need to argue with her. Know-it-alls are generally very insecure people who compensate for their sense of inadequacy by belittling others. If the know-it-all is your boss, it's best to let her feel as if she's right or even pretend that your own idea or point of view was one you got from her. That actually works more often than you might imagine. After all, it's hard for know-it-alls to conceive that *you* might have had an original thought! Your smart idea must be one of theirs that they just forgot. As long

66 99 | Advice for managers: Recognize value and wisdom.

Early in my career I had the privilege of watching a remarkable executive. It didn't matter whether he was dealing with an obnoxious client who acted as though the company should come to a grinding halt every time he called with the smallest complaint, or if he was being bullied by a corrupt union official demanding some outrageous rule change. In every case, he would listen with concentrated focus to the person who was berating, threatening, blaming, or simply unloading on him. He would never raise his voice, would always take careful notes, and would somehow find a piece of what the other party was saying that he could agree with. In almost every case, the other guy walked away feeling somewhat satisfied.

This man had the ability to make everyone feel important and respected. He always had his staff follow through on every substantive point of a conversation, and he always sent a meeting summary report to the client. The greatest thing about him was his unfailing sincerity. He did not manipulate others. He honored and respected each person's truth. He was a genius at finding favorable compromises. When people feel honored and respected, they can be disarmed. But the only way to make someone feel that way is to be sincere, and to see the value in what the other person has to say, even when his presentation is unreasonable or offensive.

as it's not too important, and it won't hurt your career, let them think that!

Then again, sometimes a know-it-all *can* affect your career by taking credit for your ideas or putting you down in front of supervisors. To protect yourself against a malignant know-it-all, calmly but firmly stand up for yourself, and make sure to let your boss know which accomplishments and ideas are yours. Explicitly challenge the know-it-all when his judgment is wrong or when he is untruthful. Don't be hostile, just clear and forceful. Ask others to back you up if necessary, if it's your word against his. Chances are, you are not the only person in your workplace the office know-it-all has belittled and irritated.

Ideally, you can take the respectful approach. Some know-it-alls appreciate your listening to them carefully and paraphrasing what they've said in a way that shows you've really heard them, especially if you convey admiration for their wisdom as you do so. Some may even be moved to listen to you in turn, so long as you don't state your case in an explicitly challenging way.

Try using statements like these:

> *"Hey, that's great! I'd like to piggyback on your idea with one suggestion."*

> *"Actually, I believe that was my idea first. Do you remember when I first brought it up, back when we were originally discussing this situation at our staff meeting? I think Mildred was there—right, Mildred?"*

> *"I really like what you're saying, and I appreciate that you know a lot about this. I have just one concern that maybe you can help address here."*

The Naysayer   A naysayer throws cold water on the most ambitious plans and brightest dreams. A naysayer will tell you, "That idea is not workable." "That's an unrealistic plan." "Ha! You're *dreaming* if you think you can do that."

The naysayer feels powerless and projects that sense of powerlessness and uselessness onto everyone else. The danger is that they can dampen other people's creativity and excitement and amplify the latent feelings of helplessness that all of us carry inside.

Arguing with a naysayer is less productive than some other approaches. Instead of negotiating or brainstorming with her, ask her to think about what she would do in lieu of what you and your team are proposing and to get back to you later. If she comes up with an alternative solution, consider it as seriously as you would if it had come from any other source. You never know, the naysayer may actually have a contribution to make. Here are some possible approaches:

> *"Can you think of a better way to do this? I'd love to get your input."*

> *"You know, I'm frustrated, too, and I'm not convinced our approach will work either. But maybe there's a way to tweak it and make it more effective. Do you have any ideas? Why not think about it a while and get back to me."*

> *"You have a point. There are some big uncertainties with this plan. Think about it and let us know if you can improve on it, and we'll table this discussion for right now."*

Naysayers are like sirens singing a song of despair. Don't let them tempt you to dash your boat on the rocks. Hold steady and keep sailing ahead, leaving the naysayer behind.

The Emotionally Clingy and Insecure Coworker

If you're a kind person, insecure coworkers may cling to you like flies. These are the people who are looking for someone to shelter them, someone they can feel protected by, or someone who will like them even if nobody else does.

At first, you don't realize what you've set yourself up for. The emotionally clingy person asks if they can carpool to work with you, and you say, "Sure!" Then they also expect that, naturally, you'll drive somewhere to lunch together every day and be best friends at work. It can happen in a thousand ways. All of a sudden, you notice you've been drafted as someone's security blanket.

Clingy coworkers are difficult to identify initially, but suddenly you realize that they like to whine a lot. "Boy, the boss was grouchy to me this morning." "The guy in the cubicle next to me made a mean joke!" "Work is just *really hard* lately. It's so good to have someone like *you* around though—someone I can really talk to."

Uh-oh. How did you get yourself into *this*?

To avoid this kind of relationship, it's best to use gentle but clear language. Don't give him a reason to feel victimized by you, and more to the point, don't set yourself up to feel guilty. Instead, devise a strategy. Remove one tentacle at a time. Say:

> *"Actually, I'd like to drive to work by myself tomorrow. I've got some things to think over."*

> *"To tell you the truth, I brought a sandwich today so that I could eat my lunch in the park and do a little reading."*

> *"You know, I think I'd like to eat in the lounge today with everyone else."*

> *"I can't really commit to driving with you every day anymore; sometimes I like to take the train."*

> *"You know, if you're unhappy with someone else's behavior around here, I think you should tell that person instead of me so you can resolve the issue."*

Slowly but surely, re-establish healthy boundaries. The clingy person may cast you baleful looks now and again, and you may even feel a twinge of guilt, but that's better than being imposed on and feeling resentful.

The Chronically Angry Coworker   Some people just simmer with anger all the time. They can't help it. They are not like passive-aggressive personalities or snipers; they *know* they are angry, but they think it's *your* fault. They bludgeon other people with angry words and snarling tones of voice. They take any occasion, use any excuse, to get angry. Being around them and trying to avoid their wrath is like tiptoeing through a minefield.

Don't get angry! It only fuels their anger and makes the situation worse. Of course, the anger isn't justified, but it isn't personal either. Calm down. Speak softly. Ask the angry person to explain again what the problem is, then repeat what you heard. If you can find a way to do so, validate her feelings. Say, "Well, I can see why that would be upsetting." Wait a bit, and then propose a solution. Angry people are generally not used to being responded to in a sincere and gracious manner.

Respectful concern may disarm their anger. Try offering words like these:

> *"It seems as if something's bothering you today. Is there anything I can do to help?"*

> *"It seems as if you're upset with me. Am I right?"*

> *"I understand your frustration with the situation. I know how you feel. It can be maddening."*

Ask careful questions. Look for common ground. As unsettling as the person's anger can be, it's just a paper tiger. If you seek mutually satisfying solutions, you might find he's more rational than you thought, at least under the surface. You might even receive an apology.

However, never tolerate physical or emotional abuse! That's a different story. If an angry person calls you names, strikes you, or threatens to hurt you in any way, that's a deal breaker. Tell your supervisor and/or Human Resources immediately. Inform your coworkers that you need to steer clear of this person, and enlist their help in doing so.

The Flagrantly Selfish Coworker

Mark was brilliant at what he did. He was so good that even his competitors enjoyed watching him work a client on the phone. He was the ultimate salesperson, born with the gift of gab. It seemed he could talk almost anyone into buying whatever he was selling. At the beginning of Mark's employment, his boss loved the work he did. But even as his star was rising in the company, the dark side of his personality was sealing his fate. Mark was one of those highly talented egomaniacs who believe the rest of us are here on Earth merely to serve him, to make his life easier so he can spread his brilliance without having a second thought for its impact on the lives of his coworkers.

Our star used up everyone around him. He always took the last cup of coffee without starting a new pot. If there were four interns in the office, he would often task each one with something to do in support of his current project. It went on like this for some time—until the nauseatingly selfish nature of his character and its impact on the rest of the office team overwhelmed his good work. The boss warned him, but Mark was set in his ways. No matter how many times he was told how toxic his habits had become to the other thirty employees in the organization, he sloughed off the criticism and refused to change. Finally, despite the strong earnings Mark brought to the firm, he was fired.

Confronting the Selfish Worker

Although Mark's case may seem exceptional, the existence of flagrantly selfish people in office environments is not unusual. If you are unfortunate enough to work with selfish individuals, you need to assert yourself. Do not allow them to take advantage of you! Most normal people make an effort to be fair and respectful, so it may seem strange to struggle against a blatantly selfish person who really doesn't care about your needs. Try to keep your distance and stay independent of them. If you work directly with them, confront them about their selfish behavior over and over again. This may be tiring to you, but it will be tiring to them as well, and eventually they will understand that you won't tolerate their games. If possible, create consequences for the selfish person. For example, if your coworker consistently leaves you with extra paperwork to do, let the boss know.

Above all, don't be afraid to call the selfish person on her selfishness. Such people need to be taken to task for their behavior, or they'll never change. Here are some ways you can approach the problem:

> *"You've left me with extra work before, and now you're doing it again. Please stop doing this. I'm going to have to report it to the boss."*

> *"You're making extra work for me, and that's causing problems. Please understand I have my own work to do, and I can't take the time to do yours as well."*

> *"You're a smart person, so you ought to realize that making extra work for me is going to upset me. Please don't do it, or I'll have to speak to the supervisor."*

Psychopaths   It goes without saying that inside or outside the workplace, the most dangerous people of all are psychopaths. I hope you never encounter one, but they are more prevalent than most people imagine.

Psychopaths have no regard whatsoever for the well-being of others and no reservation about harming other people, as long as they gain somehow from it and don't get caught. Unlike the difficult personalities discussed previously, psychopaths are beyond selfish; they are predators. Unlike the mentally ill, psychopaths are not delusional. On the contrary, they are perceptive and very much in control of themselves and their situations.

Paul Babiak is an industrial and organizational psychologist, the president of HRBackOffice, a consulting company that teaches management development, and the author of *Snakes in Suits: When Psychopaths Go to Work*. He has seen psychopaths in action in the workplace and divides them into three categories, which he described on our radio show:

THE CON, THE MANIPULATOR: This person talks a lot and uses his voice and intelligence to manipulate people, usually verbally.

THE BULLY: The bully tends to be a coarse individual who may not be as sophisticated or educated as the con and who tends to use intimidation and overt force, either physical or verbal.

THE PUPPET MASTER: The puppet master has more of the classical traits and characteristics of a psychopath than the other two types. He manipulates his direct reports, and gets them to do his dirty work.

Babiak's research further shows that psychopaths go through three phases in setting up and manipulating their prey. If you know what these phases are, you can recognize them and take action before your involvement mushrooms.

THE HONEYMOON: This is the assessment phase. While you're being enthralled by his delightful surface performance, the psychopath is busy analyzing you. You're starting to like and trust him; meanwhile, he's trying to figure out what you have that he wants and how he can get it. Over time you think you're getting to know him better, but he's only showing what he wants you to see. It is easy to convince yourself that he is who he seems to be. But what has really happened is that he has established a bond with you—which Paul Babiak calls the psychopathic bond.

THE MANIPULATION: Here's where psychopaths begin to use methods that in business we might call "impression management techniques" to get things they need and want, perhaps basics like money and sex. Or they may want different commodities, like prestige or status, or information that they'll use to get other things from other people. If you get trapped by a psychopath, you'll probably only recognize the information hustle once it's too late to avoid being victimized. In the psychopathic web, you won't see its harmful nature at first. In fact, you will be more than willing to help out your buddy, your friend, who happens to be a psychopath.

THE ABANDONMENT: Once the psychopath decides you don't have anything left to offer, he leaves you cold. He either walks away or just stops calling. If you call, he won't respond. It's as if you never existed. Only then do you begin to realize that the person you've been dealing with is not a real person but a fictional character that's been constructed for the express purpose of manipulating you. Unfortunately, you're emotionally invested at this point and hurt.

Babiak says that psychopaths usually learn how to fake mental health, which makes their psychopathology much more difficult to recognize and therapy an almost impossible challenge. The psychopath can sit next to someone who is bawling his eyes out in a therapy group and make mental notes so that she can mimic these emotions later. As Babiak explains, if the psychopath wants to come

The Psychopath as a Do-Gooder

Suppose Joan has been working with a large community nonprofit organization for the past several years. She's very proud of the organization, which operates a wide variety of programs that benefit community residents, particularly low-income families and the homeless. Joan's official title is Family Liaison. Her responsibilities include working with children from low-income families and helping them obtain the resources they need to succeed in school. She also works closely with entire families and tries to help resolve situations in the home that might negatively impact the children. Joan provides families with information about free health and counseling services in the community. Though her work is often stressful and even heartbreaking, she loves it. She knows she is making a difference in many people's lives, and she's grateful to her organization for providing the structure required for her to do her work well and make a contribution to her community.

The executive director of Joan's company, who had been there for nearly twenty years, recently retired, and the board of directors hired Fred, someone from out of state, with vast experience in community nonprofit administration and a dynamic, almost mesmerizing personality. When Fred speaks, he instills his listeners with a sense of enthusiasm and confidence. During his job interview with the board, Fred asserted that he could bring new vision and energy to the organization, which, though successful and well respected, was perhaps due for expansion in fresh directions. In particular, Fred felt that the organization could do more extensive work for homeless families, perhaps sponsoring new shelters and meal programs, even venturing into creating work opportunities. He had some very specific ideas about this, which he outlined briefly to the board, who were duly impressed.

After he was hired, Fred called a meeting to introduce himself and to meet his staff. Joan's first impressions were positive. Fred seemed genuinely friendly and humble; he seemed interested in everyone's experience and areas of interest. He posed thoughtful questions and listened carefully. He spoke with evident sincerity about how honored he was to be their new director, how he hoped he could fulfill the role, and how much he depended on their feedback and guidance. He said he looked forward to meeting with each of them privately. He also stressed his passion for helping the homeless.

His first private, face-to-face meeting with Joan was about a week later. For the first ten minutes or so, he asked Joan to describe her work with families, and he listened with rapt attention as she filled him in. Then he asked, "How many homeless families do you work with right now?"

Joan thought about it. "Actually, none. I have worked with homeless families in the past. But right now my main focus is working with families and kids from the Bartleby school district. Most homeless families don't have their kids in school."

Fred leaned back in his chair. "I see. But who do you think needs your services more—kids who have homes, or kids who don't have homes?"

Joan was confused. "Well, *my* services in particular, right now, are for kids who need help maintaining a normal school life. So I help their families, too, to give those kids the stable base they need."

Fred nodded. "And if homeless families could send their kids to school too, do you think they wouldn't do that?"

"Sure, but . . ."

"How many families are you working with now, Joan?"

"Well, it varies, because every family—"

"I mean *right now*, Joan. At this time. How many families will you be visiting this week?"

Joan hesitated. "Probably three or four."

"What about this afternoon?"

"I have to talk with a teacher at three o'clock, and—"

"So you're mostly free then?"

Joan, astonished, didn't know what to say.

"I would like you to meet the Petersons," said Fred. "They're a homeless family in Simmons Park. I can take you there myself, if you want."

"No, I don't—I mean, that won't be necessary."

Fred grinned. "I don't mind driving you. Particularly if you're at all uncomfortable going there alone."

Suddenly Joan felt very creepy and unsafe. Simmons Park was where many of the county's homeless spent their days and nights. It was a seedy place, where a lot of drug deals and drunken altercations took place. But somehow, at that moment, Joan didn't feel like she'd be any safer there with Fred.

"You can just tell me how to find them," she said. "I don't mind."

"They'll be waiting for you," said Fred. "The family is the Petersons. They have three kids. I'll call Mr. Peterson on his cell in a little while, and have him meet you by the swing set at, say, one-thirty?"

Completely befuddled, Joan could only nod. It didn't even occur to her to ask how this homeless Mr. Peterson could have a cell phone, and that Fred could have his number.

(continued)

"Great!" said Fred, flashing his trademark grin. "I'm sure it'll be a short meeting, and you'll have plenty of time to make your three o'clock. Maybe you can help get the Peterson kids set up in some type of schooling situation. I know the parents would appreciate it."

Joan met the Petersons at Simmons Park at 1:30. Mr. Peterson was a Caucasian man in his forties, with a mouthful of black teeth and a stench of alcohol about him. His gray-skinned "wife" looked no older than nineteen, and she had the vacant eyes of an addict. Mr. Peterson did all the talking in an ingratiating, wheedling tone. Joan could see immediately that he didn't care about getting his kids into school. He inquired about a "grant" from Joan's organization for himself and his family.

Joan, anxious to leave, nervously told him that she'd look into it. She left the park completely upset and called the teacher at Bartleby Elementary School to cancel her 3:00 appointment.

At the office the next day, Joan tried to avoid Fred. She succeeded, but a few days later, he entered her office and closed the door behind him. Joan was instinctively afraid.

"So how'd it go?" asked Fred with a grin.

"What?" she swallowed.

"The Petersons? Did you like them?" Fred took a step closer.

"I—Mr. Peterson asked for a 'grant' from us."

"Well, can we do that?"

"Well—we don't give 'grants' to families! That's not what we do at all!"

Fred frowned. "You mean, not what we *have* done! I suppose you don't feel the Petersons are deserving enough, being homeless and dirty?"

Joan started to shake.

"Hey," said Fred, very gently. Walking over to Joan's chair, he placed his hand on her hair and stroked her head. "Easy. I didn't mean to *upset* you. I'm just trying to get you to think outside the box. I can see you're very talented. I think you have a lot more to give than you even know."

"Thanks," croaked Joan.

"Tell you what," he said. "Obviously you have some reservations about working in a different way than you're used to. I've got a meeting in ten minutes, and then I have to go somewhere. Why don't we meet for coffee tonight after work, and we can talk about it?"

"Okay," she whispered.

"I'll pick you up here," said Fred. "Or we can just walk down to the corner place . . . what's it called? Coffee King?" He laughed.

"I think so."

"Good!" Fred gave Joan's hair one more stroke. "Don't worry about anything, all right? We'll talk about it later." And with that, he strode out of her office.

Joan sat trembling for about five minutes. Then, she grabbed her coat and her bag and left the office. The next day, she called in sick.

"So sorry to hear that," said Fred, sounding concerned. "Well, call me if you need anything!"

Joan called the chair of the board of directors, whom she had known for years and poured her heart out. She is *scared* of the new ED. She doesn't know what he wants or where he wants to take the organization, but she doesn't trust him, and she's uncomfortable going back to work.

"Well, we can't lose *you*, Joan," the board chair says. "Why don't you take a week off, and let me investigate this?"

As it turns out, Fred was moving too fast. It doesn't take the board chair long, making discreet inquiries, to discover that Joan is not his only victim. He has already significantly disrupted several programs and is apparently sleeping with at least two of the women who work at the company, both of whom are deeply embarrassed and confused by the whole thing.

So the chair calls a special meeting of the board. They ask Joan and others to submit written testimony in advance of the meeting, and they summarily vote, unanimously, to fire Fred.

In the weeks that follow, Fred threatens lawsuits; the board threatens to press charges against him for embezzlement. In fact, Fred has managed to steal a little bit of money from the organization, but not much—and the process by which he took the money is well documented. Fred has underestimated the scrupulousness of the company's personnel and accounting procedures. In the end, Fred takes his "expertise" on the road to another state.

If Fred had moved more slowly, and dug in a bit more, he might have had a chance to establish relationships and gain the trust of important donors to the organization, and even get some of his own "people" on the board of directors. That could have made it extremely difficult to unseat him without paying a terrible price. However, like many psychopaths, Fred was overconfident and overly disdainful of the integrity and moral courage of those around him. He never would have guessed, for example, that a mousy little woman

(continued)

like Joan would ever have the temerity to complain about him (her boss, the man with the power to take away her job!) to the chair of the company's board.

What motivates people like Fred is often not only money or sex but a sense of power over other people. That seems to be what he was trying to do in having Joan go to the park and meet the homeless person. Fred was trying to scare Joan to establish power over her. Fortunately, he was removed from the company before he could do permanent damage. ■

across as contrite and sincere, she now has a better picture of what that looks like to the rest of us.

Babiak clearly demonstrates that psychopaths are deceitful, dishonest people. They lie, cheat, and steal. More than that, they have no conscience. They know the difference between right and wrong, but they find the distinction amusing. They'll very easily and quickly flip from one side to the other as long as it gets them what they want in a particular situation. They feel no guilt, no empathy.

Antisocial behavior can be very normal; most of us can exhibit one or more of these traits at some time in our lives. But the real psychopath is like Dr. Jekyll and Mr. Hyde. He carries his personality disorder and antisocial behaviors with him everywhere he goes, and he can choose which side he wants you to see. To most people he meets—and certainly at the first time meeting—he presents a smooth, charming, glib, entertaining, and intelligent persona (this is, as Babiak calls it, the honeymoon phase).

Psychopaths can wreak much more than emotional pain. You might not even be aware there is a larger problem until you check your bank account and find that money has been siphoned away, your credit cards have been maxed out, or your prized possessions are missing. Worse yet, someone you love may have been harmed. Psychopaths have no moral compass, no conscience, no regard for how their actions affect others, even when the effect is to destroy people's lives and livelihoods.

Psychopaths Destroy Teams

Usually the cost to an organization is less dramatic than embezzlement, but it may also be less tangible, making it harder to identify and fix. Morale declines. Teamwork falls apart. Information isn't spread to those who need it. Conflict arises between people who worked closely together in the past and had no problems with each other . . . until now. These are the low-visibility problems that can erode and corrupt an organization. All can be the direct result of a psychopath's backstage machinations.

What do you do when you encounter a psychopath? Once you realize you're being conned and want to mend the situation, the psychopath generally initiates bullying and emotional violence. Babiak makes it clear that before blowing the whistle, you must understand your company's relevant policies. First, contact Human Resources, keeping your interaction with the department confidential. Keep in mind that you can't just call Human Resources and say, "Look, I'm working with (or for) a psychopath." HR cannot take any action based on what amounts to a subjective personality assessment. It is essential to bring forward hard data. If you have financial reports that have been doctored, for example, HR needs to see a copy of them. Whatever the case, you need to have solid ground to stand on, specific charges with examples of bad actions by the employee in question, and evidence of the negative consequences of those actions.

Fortunately, psychopaths are a rare breed compared to just about any other type of person you are likely to meet in the workplace. But as with poison oak, it's important to be able to identify them and not be lulled into complacency by their pleasant-looking shiny surfaces.

You can protect yourself by being self-aware and remembering to check your gut feelings. Psychopaths are slick but usually not as slick as they think they are. In order to fool people, psychopaths count on people to fool themselves, to ignore "funny feelings" and rationalize their reservations. It is often easier to question and doubt ourselves than to trust our perceptions and take our intuition seriously. But if you practice self-awareness and check in with your gut feelings, you're much less likely to be conned and used by a psychopath.

The Bottom Line on Difficult Coworkers

Never imagine that you can get through life avoiding difficult people. The sad fact is that they are everywhere. The good news, however, is that most people are not so

3 handling discord in the workplace

The Workplace Community

Unless you work from home, you find yourself in any work situation surrounded by people with whom you may have nothing in common but related job skills. Yet you have to get along, building and maintaining one-on-one as well as group relationships. Think of your office as a desert island where each individual has to depend on the group if any of them are to survive and make it home. Of course, this scenario usually plays out on a movie screen where you can walk out of the theater at the end of the film and shake off any lingering anxiety. But, alas, you have to return to the "theater" of your workplace every day.

Often the greatest on-the-job challenge is not the work but rather maintaining good relationships with your colleagues. When all is said and done, you probably spend about a third of your life with your coworkers. You can be friends with them, and we know that good business relationships often create a strong foundation for friendships outside work. But at some time, you're going to have conflicts with colleagues, and how you handle those conflicts will affect not only your own mental hygiene but also the mood and productivity of the entire office.

The Reality of Conflict

Your coworkers make up a large part of your landscape. The day-to-day frictions and challenges of completing the tasks you're assigned create an undercurrent of stress

47

that, like spilled milk, spreads quickly and can leave a nasty stain.

We tend to think about conflicts as being between two people, but that's not always the case. Conflict can happen among several people in a group or between groups in different departments. There even—and let's hope this never happens to you—can be battles across an entire organization, such as when a company is being rocked by some internal scandal that divides people's opinions and loyalties.

Sometimes conflict can be a good thing. When handled intelligently, skillfully, and without hostility, conflict can challenge ideas, solve problems, promote growth, and defy personal obstacles. Disagreement often means that options are studied more thoroughly, which leads to smarter decisions and better business. It's healthy when people can agree to disagree then disagree in a civil, productive fashion. That kind of disagreement gives rise to dialogue and negotiation, leading to agreement and shared success.

Embrace Productive Conflict

Unfortunately, many people see all disagreement as destructive and therefore shy away from it. They suppress their feelings to avoid conflict at all costs. They assume that conflict has to be messy and unpleasant, and that by avoiding it they can keep the peace. Or they fear retribution, ostracism, and ridicule from coworkers if they express their dissent.

Believe it or not, if you avoid productive conflict, your mental health will suffer. Conflict may be avoidable in some situations, but it's inevitable that at one point or another, discord will arise in the workplace. Why else are mediation services a booming industry? It is important to learn to handle conflict constructively.

Fighting Fair

Let's begin with the fundamental rules of fair, intelligent conflict.

1. **DON'T CALL PEOPLE NAMES.** This may seem obvious, but even mature adults can resort to this when things get heated. Does this sound familiar? "You're being pigheaded and narrow minded!" "You just don't get it!" "You only care about yourself." "You don't know what you're talking about!" "That's ridiculous!" Okay, technically speaking, none of these abusive statements (and yes, I do mean abusive) contain a name. But it's all name-calling nonetheless, and it's not productive. Have you ever heard of a bestselling self-help book entitled "Using Unflattering Characterizations to Persuade Others and Get Your Way"? No, neither have I. Remember the old saying, "Sticks and stones may break my bones, but names will never hurt me." Well, it's nonsense, as any first-grader can tell you. And as I'm sure you know yourself.

2. **KEEP THE CONFLICT AWAY FROM PERSONALITIES.** The bottom line is that it is imperative to communicate respectfully. In addition to not attacking the other person's character or competence, do not threaten drastic consequences should you fail to win an argument. And don't dredge up the other person's misdeeds or mistakes from the past. This is also unfair and will not score you any debate points.

3. **BE WILLING TO QUESTION YOUR OWN POINT OF VIEW AND TO ENTERTAIN OPTIONS OTHER THAN YOUR OWN.** There aren't just two sides to any conflict; there are usually at least three or four. Keep an open mind, and don't assume that you're operating from divinely revealed knowledge.

4. **DON'T WORRY SO MUCH ABOUT WINNING THE CONFLICT.** Remember the big picture. What are you ultimately trying to accomplish? It may well be that your adversary has the same ultimate goal as you have, whether it's completing a project well or simply getting along. Identify your common ground, and affirm it with your words.

5. **FIND SOMETHING TO PRAISE IN YOUR OPPONENT'S POSITION.** Acknowledge the merit of what he is saying. But be sincere, don't just try to butter him up or it will backfire. The only thing more alienating than being called names is being

transparently patronized. When you call your coworker a name, he will most likely understand that you want to make him feel dumb. But when you try to manipulate him with honey-coated phrases, then he believes that you must really *think* he is dumb!

Jealousy and Competition

Two of the primary causes of workplace conflict are competition and jealousy. Jealousy can cause conflict in any situation, but it's particularly volatile at work when coworkers see each other winning coveted promotions, or enjoying the positive regard of a mutual supervisor, or even flirting with the same person.

Jealousy can fester and grow more poisonous over time. One of the hardest things about jealousy is that it's not an easy emotion to be forthcoming and honest about. If the person in the cubicle next to you talks too loudly on the phone, you can politely ask her to speak a little softer. But if your coworker routinely goes out to lunch with your best friend and you're not invited, well, what's your complaint exactly, and to whom will you address it?

Worse yet, jealousies conceived in the workplace are inescapable. You have to confront them every day. You can't take a vacation from the dynamic that's causing the jealousy.

You can, however, try noticing what you're feeling and accept it; treat yourself with compassion. Then you can ask yourself if the object of your jealousy is that important. Does it matter that the boss and your obnoxious coworker both root for the Philadelphia Eagles and like to shoot the breeze about football and other topics that don't interest you? Do you *really* want to go out with that attractive person who seems to have a crush on your colleague? Well, maybe you do, but there are lots of nice-looking fish in the sea, possibly even another interesting fish or two in your work-a-day fishbowl.

The Dishonest Arguer

The BUSINESS Shrink

*Say Shirley calls me from Chicago and asks, "What do I do if I'm having a conflict with somebody who's really *smart* and good with words but who isn't *honest*? I mean, what if this person doesn't really care about the truth of the matter but only about justifying himself and putting me down? I can be reasonable and respectful, I can state my point of view and try to be open-minded, but he isn't doing any of that. He's taking every concession I make as a weakness."

"That's a tough situation, Shirley," I admit. "It's hard to stay steady in the face of an onslaught of words from someone who's good at arguing but not good at being real. Here's my advice: Work around him. Do your job well, make sure other people know you're doing your job well, make sure other people are aware of your situation, and get support from your coworkers and your supervisor. Don't argue with him. Let your boss know that you don't feel you can work with this guy. You don't have to justify yourself. Chances are other people in the office have had the exact same experience with him that you have."

In a situation like Shirley's, your coworkers can be your best allies. Often they can give useful advice about handling a difficult or unpleasant colleague. The important thing is not to get drawn into this person's arena. Just back away from it, because you can't win when you fight on his terms. But with the support of your boss and your coworkers, you can isolate him and limit the damage he does.

FOLLOW-UP: A WEEK LATER

Shirley calls back to say she's figured out what to do. "You were right," she tells me. "I don't have to argue with him. In fact, if I don't let him hook me, if I don't get defensive, it seems to defuse him. All he's really after is an emotional reaction from me."

ME: Well, he certainly sounds like an unpleasant guy, if all he's interested in is making trouble for you just for the hell of it.

SHIRLEY: Oh, it's not like that. He doesn't even know what he's doing. He's compulsive about it. When I take a step back, I can see that he doesn't know how to get along with people, so fighting is the only way he knows how to keep people involved. As long as I respond to him, even if I get angry, he gets fed because I'm paying him attention.

ME: So you're saying that this guy is really starved for attention?

SHIRLEY: That's what I've figured out, yeah. And he hasn't got a healthy way of getting it. So he gets mean. It's pathetic really. He's no threat to me anymore. ∎

Be Your Own Person

The key to fixing problems with jealousy is to remember that comparing yourself with others is not productive, helpful, or illuminating. You are your own person; you're running your own race, walking your own path. Everybody has strengths and weaknesses. The person you are jealous of may have problems you can't even begin to imagine, so count your blessings!

Competition is even more common than jealousy. How could there not be competition at work? Comparisons are inevitable when more than one person is doing more or less the same job. Of course everybody wants to look as good and achieve as much as the next person.

Like conflict, competition can be healthy or unhealthy, and it's crucial to understand the difference. Unhealthy competition is mean-spirited and cutting. It's you or your colleague, and you'll do whatever you have to do to make sure you win. Unhealthy competition often involves underhanded tactics like trying to make your opponent look bad or putting him down behind his back.

A Trip to Manila— What Is It Worth to You?

Unhealthy competition also induces people to grab unfair advantage when they can. For example, suppose the boss has to decide to take either you or your co-worker along on an upcoming business trip to the Philippines. The stakes are high. The company that you'd be visiting is a potential business partner, and whoever accompanies the boss will be functioning as something of an ambassador to this company. Besides, you've never seen Manila, and you'd love to go.

Now let's say the boss has presented some crucial information at a staff meeting, which your coworker missed due to illness. Under normal circumstances, you would bring her up-to-date on the important details of the meeting. In the past, your relationship has been cordial, and you've depended on each other for this type of support and numerous other acts of consideration. But in this instance, you can put the information you gained at the meeting to use in a manner that would make you a more attractive candidate for the business trip. Besides she'll never know if you don't tell her about it. If she asks you what transpired at the staff meeting, you can just tell her "truthfully" about matters that were discussed but leave out the key data.

What's wrong with this picture? Several things.

On the one hand, if your coworker doesn't know certain information but you do, you can gain an advantage, keep the information from her, and grab the prize!

On the other hand, what if she finds out about the staff meeting from somebody else? What if—after she talks to you—she realizes that you've deliberately withheld information? Then you'll have an enemy, or at least you'll have forfeited her trust indefinitely. If you continue to work together for years, your compromised relationship could make life distinctly less pleasant around the office.

What if she *does* get to go to Manila instead of you? Won't there be similar opportunities in the future? If you help her obtain the tools and knowledge she needs to have a fair shake at this, maybe she'll remember and help *you* look good at some critical point down the road. If you go instead of her, even after having helped her, she'll be much more likely to wish you well and less likely to feel resentful or jealous.

Check in with your emotions. On the one hand, you *want* to go on that trip! But if you're self-aware, you may realize you have other feelings as well. You might feel a bit guilty and a little ashamed if you sell your coworker short. You might feel a little anxious about the whole thing—the trip and your deception.

Healthy Competition   Healthy competition requires you to listen to all your emotions. Healthy competition takes the attitude that "there's enough to go around." One way or another, if you don't grab the brass ring this time because somebody else was in front of you, it will certainly come around again, and you will have your turn. Healthy competition recognizes that you share important goals and values with the people you're competing against and that these common interests are generally more important and longer lasting than the things you're competing for.

When you're engaged in healthy competition, you and your opponents inspire each other to excel. It's not a matter of tearing each other down. It's about prodding each other to stretch beyond your limits and discover your capabilities. In the end, win or lose, healthy competition strengthens you, sets a new bar for what you can achieve, and leaves you with heightened self-confidence and self-esteem.

Mutual respect is the key to healthy competition. In the scenario described earlier, telling your coworker about what she missed at the meeting is an expression of respect as well as honesty and consideration. You respect her abilities, you respect the job she does, and you want to honor her talents not exploit her weaknesses. It's a matter of self-respect as well. Can you compete while maintaining your dignity and integrity? Can you take satisfaction in the successes of others? If you can, then competition is a win–win situation.

A healthy attitude about competition is essential to maintaining an atmosphere of basic trust in the workplace. In the words of Peter F. Drucker, author of *Management Challenges for the 21st Century* and more than a dozen other outstanding books on organization and business culture, "Organizations are no longer built on force. They are increasingly built on trust. Trust does not mean that people like one another. It means that people can trust one another."

Conflict   Not all conflict can be resolved by taking the high road.
Management   Sometimes personalities simply don't get along, misunderstandings happen, or people are just rude, inconsiderate,

or even malicious. You can't begin to resolve a conflict until you diffuse it, and the first step is to depersonalize it. Focus on the issues involved, not the personalities. Even if the other guy is being mercenary, don't take it personally. It's really not about you.

Unhooking Conflict   Katherine Crowley, a psychotherapist and author of the book *Working with You Is Killing Me*, refers to the process of diffusing and depersonalizing conflict as *unhooking*. As she explained on our radio show, "Unhooking comes from the notion that when someone else's behavior really bothers you, whether it's the nasal tone in their voice or the fact that they may have just singled you out in a meeting and yelled at you, then we actually get hooked. We churn up emotionally and obsess about the situation, and it prevents us from doing our work well. If you can unhook, that is, if you take steps to change your internal reaction and figure out the business actions available to you, then you can actually change the outcome of the conflict as well as the dynamic with the other person involved."

Crowley suggested that if you are conscious of the results, and you want to take charge of your emotions, you can employ the following four techniques to do so.

1. **UNHOOK PHYSICALLY.** Start with the simplest and most direct approach, which is the body. You have to cool the system down. Start by taking a moment to recognize what's happening to you physically, that you're in an intersection of emotions as complex as an L.A. freeway interchange during rush hour. Take some deep breaths. Take some more deep breaths. It's amazing how much can get resolved, how quickly your whole state of being can be altered, just by engaging in some conscious breathing. You can try other techniques, too, besides deep breathing. Splash water on your face, walk around the block, or work out at the gym for an hour. If there's something that's really

tearing you up inside, unhooking yourself physically is the best first step.

2. **UNHOOK MENTALLY**. Follow that physical action with mental unhooking. Once you've cooled your body's reactions, try to look at your situation from a clear perspective. Crowley recommends that you ask yourself the following questions to aid in the unhooking process:

- What's going on here?
- What are the facts?
- What did the other person actually do that upset me?
- What did I do?
- What were my actions, and now what are my real options?

Mentally unhooking means using the logical part of your mind to connect with the feeling part of your mind—in effect internally verbalizing that you know you are feeling a certain way. For example, "I know that I am mad. I know that I am hurt." That awareness of your feelings doesn't mean you have to act out a personal response. It means knowing that as bad as a situation may feel, the person you're in conflict with may also be in pain, and it's not really personal to you, so you need not respond personally.

3. **UNHOOK VERBALLY**. Next in Crowley's process, you need to get outside your body and mind. What are some of the things you can say to improve your situation? Don't assume the other person will change his or her position or take the initiative to resolve things. You can only move forward if you say something—and not something snide or antagonistic. If you've made it to the third step, you're already looking for and maybe have found ways to de-escalate. Now it's time to express them.

4. **UNHOOK PROFESSIONALLY**. Finally, because we're talking about workplace relationships and the resources of an organization are at your disposal, Crowley points out that you can

unhook by using business tools. That could mean a simple memo or e-mail to memorialize an agreement in writing, following up with action, documenting someone else's behavior, or referring to policies and procedures. It depends on the situation, of course. This fourth step is critical, because it actually translates the crisis from something personal and intangible into something concrete that you and your coworkers and managers can hold on to and act upon in a positive and productive manner.

Healthy Conflict Resolution   Do not try to repress conflict; in the long run it will cost you emotionally. We have all met people—and maybe you've experienced this—who go to work every day with a knot in their stomach, a literal pain in their neck, or heightened blood pressure due to impending conflict. Without fail, unresolved conflicts of a serious nature become poison.

The first thing to do to cope with conflict is to depersonalize the situation. Refer back to Katherine Crowley's advice for unhooking to depersonalize the conflict step by step.

Frame potentially confrontational communication in a positive light. Remember the principles of healthy competition? The same ones apply to healthy disagreement. Differences of opinion are a resource, not a bottleneck.

Understand your emotions before you state your positions, opinions, and feelings. Particularly if you are in a supervisory role, clear your mind before you announce controversial orders, critiques, or evaluations. But regardless of your place in the hierarchy, try to eliminate any emotional contaminants from your interactions with colleagues.

Put yourself in your coworkers' shoes, and understand how what you say and do is received by them, regardless of your intent. Remember that it's not just what you say but what people hear that counts. Observe yourself carefully, and watch the words you choose. Practice empathy for the person on the other side of the table. As Dan Goleman states in *Working with Emotional Intelligence,* "The ultimate act of personal responsibility at work may be in taking control of our own state of mind."

State Your Needs   I saved this one for last because it may be the most important tool for avoiding and diffusing conflict.

In any conflict situation—or in *any* situation, for that matter—more often than not you will get a positive response if you can clearly identify and state what you need from the other person. More important, by facing conflict head-on, you'll be a happier person, improve your relationship with your coworkers, and generally experience *less* conflict.

We often expect people to be mind readers. We wait for someone to notice that something is bothering us rather than speaking up for ourselves. While we wait for others to intuit our needs, though, we remain unsatisfied and build up resentment.

You are far more likely to get what you want if you express your feelings and needs. It is essential to assert yourself and be direct when it comes to workplace issues.

Knowing what you need and being able to communicate it clearly is a skill that you can develop over time, as you practice self-awareness. Ultimately, it's one of the keys to any successful ongoing relationship.

A Troubled   In the previous chapter we talked about how to handle
Atmosphere   some difficult personality types. While these strategies can be very effective in one-on-one situations, they unfortunately cannot address the effect that difficult people tend to have *on an entire office culture.*

The saying "One bad apple spoils the barrel" is apt here. It does not take more than one or two toxic personalities to poison the atmosphere for everyone. For example,

When your team members fail to meet expectations or do an otherwise less-than-adequate job, consequences must follow. For those of us who hate to make people feel bad, this is the most difficult part of management.

Berating an employee is out of the question. There is *never* an excuse to be abusive. Even when you feel you must let someone go, you can do so without rancor and with sincere regret (if you have any, that is).

Between mild dissatisfaction with and dismissing an employee, there lies a vast and fertile territory of opportunity for correction. It is crucial, then, that every supervisor understand and practice the basic principles of constructive criticism. Before speaking with your employee, make sure that you have your facts straight and that criticism is necessary. If you are not diligent about this process and mistakenly assume that the employee is at fault for something he did not do, you run the risk of making your employee feel persecuted.

Next, have a discussion with your employee about the deed, lapse of judgment, failure to follow through, or pattern of behavior that has brought about this conversation. Don't speak in general terms about any character deficits. Be concrete, and frame the problem so that it is clear you are not unfavorably disposed to the person but only to this particular behavior. Affirm that you value his contribution to the team.

FIND A POSITIVE OUTCOME

Offer solutions and suggest clear steps that can be taken to correct his behavior or to avoid the same mistake in the future. Find out what the person's concerns are and what special circumstances, if any, contributed to the problem.

Talk about why it is essential to the goals of the team or the mission of the organization that this problem be corrected. Don't assume that your employee understands the impact of his mistakes or the importance of his role in your department.

Assure him that you have confidence in him and envision a positive outcome to the situation. Describe the positive outcome you desire, and ask for his agreement. Always express yourself with respect. As a supervisor, you are the person most responsible for upholding the standard of respect in your environment.

When I am angry or annoyed with one of my employees for not thinking something through carefully and thoroughly, meeting a deadline, not doing what I asked, or not coming up with the quality of work I expect, I sit down with her and explain the problem. I try to mentor her, explaining the difficulties I see with her work, then brainstorming and collaborating on ways to improve. I also offer detailed guidelines, set new deadlines, and work with my team member to improve her efforts.

Michael Feiner puts it well in *The Feiner Points of Leadership*: "Feedback is a gift, in two ways. It's a gift to the recipient, because it provides data that can allow him or her to improve performance. But it's also a gift to the feedback giver himself or herself. By giving feedback that helps enhance the performance of the subordinate, the leader helps ensure that the unit's overall performance will improve."

when you have a grumpy or irritable interaction, it affects your disposition toward the next person you speak with. Even if just one person in the room is mean and cutting, no one feels comfortable.

Worse yet, sometimes a difficult person's mindset is contagious. Unconsciously, other people in the office start adopting negative attitudes and behaviors, perhaps not to the same degree as the "problem personality," but enough to degrade the atmosphere of the workplace.

Mean Gossip   One common, insidious form of dysfunctional behavior in the workplace is gossip. But gossip is not easy to define. On the one hand, it's natural for people to talk about each other. "Hey, did you hear John got that promotion?" "Mary had her baby on Saturday! Isn't that great?" There is nothing inherently malicious or destructive about this type of talk; it can be a way to affirm that the workplace is indeed a community. But take it one step further—"John sure kissed a lot of butt to make *that* happen!" "Do you suppose Mary and her husband will try something other than the rhythm method now that she's popped out her fifth kid? They sure are helping to overpopulate the planet!"—and before you know it, you're in corrupt territory. The intention is no longer to celebrate the good fortune of your friends; now you're taking them down a notch. This is mean gossip.

Gossip is even worse when it involves spreading false rumors or making derogatory insinuations. You probably remember the game of "telephone" from when you were a kid: The first person whispers something into the second person's ear, the second person whispers the same message to the third person, and so on until you get to about the twentieth person who tells the group what the last person told her. It always turns out to be appreciably different from the original statement. That's an illustration of what happens with the spreading of *neutral* information. Something always is misinterpreted or reframed in a misleading way. Add to that the element of ill intent and even a slight exaggeration or unkind implication can mushroom into a slander campaign that damages reputations and causes irreparable harm, not just to one person but to an entire workplace culture.

Furthermore, with the advent of e-mail and electronic communication, gossip spreads faster than ever. You may think you're only telling one person, but *watch out!* As Michael Feiner cautions in *The Feiner Points of Leadership*, "Keep the gossip until you get home and then tell your cat. *If you're not willing to see it on the bulletin board or in an e-mail, don't say it and don't write it.*"

When Others Gossip

Okay. But what if the problem is not you? What if you've been fastidious about avoiding gossipy conversations, even saying, "I'm not comfortable talking behind someone's back"? What if, despite your own trustworthiness, one or two socialites in your office make gossip much too tempting for most of your coworkers to resist? And as a result, your office is not such a safe place. You never know whether they've been talking about *you*. You don't know how to interpret the occasional funny look, sideways smile, or downward glance. And nobody else does either. This kind of interpersonal edginess diminishes morale and erodes teamwork. It's a distraction from getting things done, because it gives employees something else to worry about in their day-to-day work life. Who's the fall guy today? What's the rumor mill churning up now? Is it my turn?

How Do You Deal with Gossip?

First, you must maintain your own integrity and *never* participate in mean gossip. If you've gossiped once or twice already, okay, you're human. We all do that. But don't do it again. It's a peculiar equation, but it's true: *the less you gossip, the less you will feel threatened by others' gossip.*

People are always interested in each other's lives; there is no escaping that. But keep talking about others to a minimum, even if it's innocent. When you do talk about coworkers who are not present, make sure you're not motivated by competition or vindictiveness. It's important to assess your own motives before you open your mouth.

If the gossiping has gotten out of hand, it might be appropriate to bring up the issue at a team meeting. Better yet, discreetly ask your boss to do it. (But don't tell your boss who is gossiping! *That* would be the worst *kind* of gossip!) You may find that you're not the only one who has been concerned about the level of gossip. Others may be relieved that the subject is finally being aired with everyone together. A frank team discussion about the ramifications of gossip in the office can create a clean slate, with group members newly aware of the consequences of gossip and committed to more responsible speech.

If you become aware of a false rumor about someone that is starting to circulate, take the initiative to *nip it in the bud*. Don't pretend it has nothing to do with you. If you're aware of it, it's your responsibility. What if it was your reputation on the line, and others stood by and let it be tarnished? Confront the false rumor head-on. When you hear it alluded to or spoken of—even if you just *overhear* it—stop the conversation in its tracks and say, "Hey, I know for a fact that is not true." If there is one person in particular who insists on perpetuating a false rumor, then confront that person directly, preferably in the presence of others. "I've heard you say that more than once now. But I'm afraid you're mistaken. It's just not true." Be careful. Don't get righteous. As hard as it may seem, you have to be humble and respectful—though firm—about debunking false rumors.

Be the Antigossip   Finally, you can help improve a gossipy atmosphere by promoting thoughtful conversation, respectful listening, and well-intentioned words. Assume that nearly everyone prefers a healthy, supportive social environment to a backbiting snake pit. Model and encourage positive speech. For example, if someone says something complimentary about a third person, you could say, "That's really perceptive of you to notice that. Now that you mention it, I see what you mean." But be sincere! Don't try too hard to do this or you risk looking like Pollyanna. Don't cast yourself as a cheerleader for "good vibes." Just be on the lookout for small opportunities to reinforce honorable communication.

An Edge in the Air   Gossip can give rise to a stressful work environment, but so can irritable, angry people. When the amount of negativity in an office reaches a critical mass, everyone feels it, and the air crackles with nervous tension. You may have your own tools for dealing with the naysayer, the know-it-all, or the sniper, but sometimes these personality types can infect an entire office with nastiness and short tempers. Little things get blown up. No one has patience with others' mistakes. The smallest obstacles cause enormous irritation. To make matters worse, everyone thinks they have to tiptoe around the one person who chronically acts like a walking plastic explosive.

If you're dealing with an office that's on edge, look around. No, it isn't just you. See Sally over there chewing her nails. See Len tapping his fingers against his mouse pad in a nervous, staccato fashion. See the boss scowling as if he'd like to find someone to spill his coffee on but can't decide who.

So it's not you. Take a deep breath. We're all in this together. Calm your mind. Smile if you can.

Make an effort to be pleasant to coworkers. If you're going down the hall to get some coffee, ask someone nearby if she'd like you to bring her a cup as well. Ask people how they're doing. Make eye contact.

If it's appropriate, try to "call" what's happening. Say, "Is it me or are we all a little uptight today?" Try and introduce humor into the situation when you can. Laughter lightens tension.

A Toxic Problem

June started work at Sylvia's accounting firm. June has plenty of professional experience. She is a tremendously hard worker, her work is first-rate, and she always meets deadlines. The problem is she's snappish and cold. She seems to radiate the attitude that she's too good to be there, as if everyone else is a peon.

Ask June the simplest question, and she seems irritated. Sometimes she rushes around the office for no apparent reason, looking as though she might run you down if you get in her way. She doesn't make eye contact. Everybody else tenses up a bit when June is in the room. What used to be a relaxed, collegial office is now a stressful, clamped-down environment. Nobody knows how to deal with her.

Soon people begin talking about June behind her back. What a witch she is! They wonder how her husband can stand her. Does she have children? Boy, what a misfortune it would be to have a mother like June! Who does she think she is anyway? Look at her! She actually has her nose in the air!

Then when June walks into the room, people look away, because they've been talking about her. June senses this, and it makes her even more furious than usual, but she doesn't say anything. Soon she begins acting out in more dramatic ways. She starts slamming doors. She bangs things on her desk, sending small shockwaves through the office.

Everyone's work starts to suffer, at first a little bit and then a lot. No one can concentrate. Even relations with clients are brittle and tense. There is no sense of ease in the office anymore.

A NEEDED CONVERSATION

Finally, Sylvia, the boss, approaches June, and asks her to come into her office for a private talk.

"June," says Sylvia. "You've been working here for a couple of months now. I'm wondering, how do you like it?"

"I'm fine," June answers tersely.

"Well," says Sylvia. "You certainly do fine work. But I've noticed that you seem a little unhappy. You look angry. Does anybody here do anything that bothers you?"

"No. I'm fine."

"Do you like working around other people, June?"

"Sure. It doesn't matter. I can also work well when I'm alone."

"Do you dislike the people here? Answer me honestly. I know you're not happy, and I need to know why."

June grimaces. "It's not that. I know people don't like me, and it's my fault. But I'm afraid to tell you what's bothering me because nothing can be done about it."

Sylvia leans forward and puts her chin on her hands. "Well, spit it out then. Don't keep me in suspense. I promise you have nothing to lose by telling me."

June glances downward. She seems to be trying to choose words carefully. "It's kind of a health issue," she says slowly.

"Are you ill?" asks Sylvia immediately.

"Well, no. I mean, at least not yet."

Sylvia folds her arms. "June, you have something to tell me. Please just say it."

SOMETHING JUST SMELLS

"It's . . . it's the *disinfectant* or something in here," June says. "It's overpowering. Every day I come in, and it assaults my senses. I can't understand why other people don't notice. I'm sure it's toxic."

"The disinfectant? You mean the smell of the cleaning supplies? Like, the stuff they use to clean the carpet each week?"

"I guess. I just find it *intolerable*. I can't *understand* how you've all been working in this . . . chemical fog. I'm sorry, I don't want to quit, but . . . since you asked . . . now I told you."

Sylvia leans back in her chair. "I guess the smell *is* strong now that you mention it," she admits. "I just don't tend to notice those things. And I can open a window in here."

"My office window doesn't open," June points out.

Sylvia nods. "Most of the windows are painted shut. Maybe we can do something about that."

So Sylvia brings up the issue of the cleaning smell at the next staff meeting. Guess what? It's not only June who's noticed it. Lots of people were bothered by it, but no one had felt strongly enough to say anything.

They discussed different options. They could get someone to reopen their windows, and let the place air out a bit more during the day. Or they could ask the janitor about the products being used to clean the carpet, and maybe

(continued)

see about affecting a switch. Either way, getting to the bottom of June's negativity is clearly going to benefit everyone in the office. Sylvia gives June due credit at the staff meeting for bringing up the issue of the pervasive cleaning odor.

Isn't it funny? All along, June wasn't mad about her coworkers. She was mad about something in the environment. She had her "nose in the air" because she was unconsciously trying to escape the smell!

As a new employee, June was hesitant to criticize a part of the environment that no one else seemed to even notice, much less mind. Luckily, Sylvia demonstrated some empathy in getting June to finally talk. As Dan Goleman wrote in *Working with Emotional Intelligence*, "Being able to pick up on such emotional clues is particularly important in situations where people have reason to conceal their true feelings—a fact of life in the business world." ■

If a particularly irritable person terrorizes your office, be a model of strong behavior toward her. Don't shrink when she walks by. Keep eye contact. If she snaps at you, say, "It's not necessary to snap. If you need something, please tell me respectfully." Let her know you're not intimidated.

Above all, when there's an edge in the air, break out of it. Even if the office is running on stress, you are not obligated to do the same. If it's a chronic situation, it may be worth bringing up in a team meeting. Stress does not help work get done more efficiently.

Defensiveness and Paranoia

One of the worst consequences of having passive-aggressive personalities, snipers, and selfish coworkers around is that they nip at you, manipulate you, or bludgeon you into feeling insecure at work. They create an atmosphere in which everyone feels they have to defend themselves against unpredictable and unfair attacks and power maneuvers in the office.

Paranoia can be paralyzing. How do you focus on your creative task when you're afraid that someone may steal your work? How can you relax when you think your colleagues is waiting to pounce on your next mistake so he can look good?

In an office atmosphere characterized by paranoia and defensiveness, people are worried about surviving in their jobs. This fear poisons collegiality and team spirit. Everyone thinks they have to prove themselves or defend themselves; therefore, people are busy "looking out for number one" and no one can spare too much thought or energy for the team's mission.

If you're stuck in a paranoid, fear-driven work environment, you can do something. You might even be able to turn it around, for yourself and your coworkers.

The Power of Generosity

To begin with, be generous. Whenever possible, without damaging or compromising yourself, go out of your way to make others look good. Praise other people's achievements in public. Do what you can to make others' accomplishments more visible. Better yet, again without compromising your own situation, cover for your colleagues' mistakes when you can, and when it seems reasonable to do so. (That is, don't cover for anyone's *chronic* incompetence or laziness.) This alleviates the need for defensiveness, and somebody may do a favor for you next week.

If there is a particular person who is single-handedly causing much of the office paranoia by behaving in selfish, mercenary, underhanded ways, take steps to expose this person. We said in Chapter 2 that it is best to avoid selfish coworkers when possible, unless you have to work with them directly. But if you have a colleague who is clearly

66 99 | **Advice for managers:** Show emotion, but not fear.

Just because you sit in the commander's seat, you don't have to park your emotions at the door. But you do have to regulate how you express them. It's normal to be fearful on occasion. Sharing your fears with your subordinates, however, is not appropriate.

Robin Wolaner, author of *Naked in the Boardroom: A CEO Bares Her Secrets So You Can Transform Your Career* and former CEO of Sunset Publishing, put it this way to our listeners: "As a manager, and certainly as a CEO, if you're not feeling any fear then you're not paying attention. You should know that you're afraid, you should recognize it, and you should make sure that you're making smart decisions in response to it. But if you're the leader, I don't think sharing that fear is usually productive." Wolaner explained that if you have people reporting to you, your power to motivate is essential. You are the source of the collective will to go forward, and showing your fear will not further this aim.

Think about it. You like it when an airline pilot uses that laconic, no-sweat voice to tell you, "There is some turbulence ahead, but we've got it covered." What you don't want is for him to accidentally open his microphone to the passenger cabin and be overheard saying to his copilot, "Gee, Harry, we're pretty boxed in here. I hope we make it to Cleveland before we run out of gas in that tornado up ahead!"

having a negative effect on the entire office, regardless of whether you're forced to have much direct contact with this person, you can and should try to mitigate the effects of her actions by drawing public attention to specific instances of her misbehavior. This public attention may be in the form of a statement at a meeting or something you point out to coworkers in some other setting. But make sure you are not descending into gossip. A good rule of thumb is to make sure that the selfish coworker is *present* when you state your observation. It's also best if you can make your statement a positive, not a negative, affirmation.

Finally, talk to your coworkers and your boss about the problems you perceive in the office atmosphere. A team meeting is often a good place to do this. (There is no need to point fingers in a general discussion about the "feeling in the air.") Brainstorm ways to make it better. There is no need to "go it alone." Chances are strong that if you perceive you're working in a diseased atmosphere, you're not the only one who sees it that way.

Greed and Ruthless Competition

Another symptom of a dysfunctional work environment is an entrenched pattern of cut-throat competition for promotions, choice assignments, or even just the boss's attention. Healthy competition is fine, as we discussed earlier. But the presence of a few difficult personalities can ratchet up the intensity of competition for all concerned and can give rise to an office culture in which everyone is greedy to "score" for themselves, even if it's at the expense of others.

This is a dangerous situation because the stakes are real and very high. Hatred and resentment can fester and corrode the workplace. In this type of situation, people see their coworkers as foes, not friends.

The best way to proceed in a situation like this is very carefully! You don't want to step on any land mines, and you don't want someone to cheat you out of the credit or reward for your hard work. Yet, you don't want to contribute to the rancor and hostility of the environment. So what do you do?

Try some of the same strategies that were suggested earlier for countering paranoia and defensiveness. Be a little generous. Help others to succeed when that's feasible. Build alliances with like-minded coworkers who also want to change the atmosphere. If you trust and respect your boss, go to him or her with your concerns about what's going on.

Work with your boss and coworkers to establish standards of civility and fairness. Do this publicly at meetings or via memos. You might be the first one to bring up this idea, but you won't be arriving at solutions alone. What parameters can you suggest for office behaviors that would make everyone feel a bit safer? What kinds of behaviors can you identify (without pointing fingers or naming names) that have caused you and others to feel slighted or unfairly "edged out" in the past? What types of goals should employees set for themselves, and what minimal considerations should they be expected to show one another?

A Culture of Distrust   This is really the bottom line. All other workplace dysfunctions point to this one: distrust. Unfair competition, defensiveness, paranoia, backbiting, and gossip are all forms of distrust and untrustworthy behavior. Trust is the backbone of a healthy work environment, and distrust is the cancer that eats away at it. In the words of Michael Feiner, "Trust is the single most important element of peer-to-peer relationships. It's the foundation for productive feedback being given and received, it's the antidote to reflexive and destructive assumptions of a partner's incompetence. . . . And trust, like reputations and like stock markets, can lose ninety percent of its value overnight. Or, as a former student once told me, trust is like virginity: you only lose it once!"

Above all, be trustworthy. Act in ways that you respect yourself for (and demand no less from coworkers). This means being honest, being fair, not talking behind other people's backs, working to get ahead on merit, not allowing other people to be unfairly taken advantage of, striving to further yourself in an honest and transparent fashion, and supporting the efforts of your office mates.

When you have relationships that are blessed by mutual trust, treat them preciously. Honor them, and know that

66 99   **Advice for managers:** Build teamwork and trust.

As a manager, it falls primarily to you to build a culture of trust. The values that characterize an organizational culture tend to trickle down from the top.

Build trust within your office or work group by fostering teamwork. Begin by clarifying that teamwork and collaboration are not optional. Form teams to solve problems. Have your workers set up their own team meetings. Find ways to emphasize that you all depend on each other. Set up group rewards for outstanding collective achievements. Make sure that teamwork is publicly recognized and rewarded, so that stories about team successes become part of the water cooler chatter and company folklore.

Honor special occasions in employees' lives, such as birthdays or weddings. While you don't want to invite the messy complexity of everyone's personal life into the workplace, it does makes sense to show, when appropriate, that you care about your workers as people and recognize that they do have lives and life stories outside work.

Also important is to demonstrate sympathy, concern, and support when an employee suffers a family crisis, serious illness, or accident. At a staff meeting, brainstorm ideas to help the stricken person. A sense of shared responsibility for an afflicted coworker will also reinforce team spirit.

As John P. Kotter states in his book, *Leading Change,* "In a fast-moving world, teamwork is enormously helpful almost all the time."

they are ultimately of far more value to you than mere approval or admiration.

Work on building trust with coworkers. Show them that you are trustworthy in your actions and words. Work against distrust by conducting yourself impeccably, and inspiring others to emulate you.

Try Not to Take It Personally . . . Even Though It's All Personal

I said in my introductory chapter that all business is personal. And it is—intensely so, especially when you're dealing with people face to face. You can't help but interpret coworkers' expressions, and imagine what they might mean in relation to you. Then there's the sense of smell! Consciously or unconsciously, we all pick up on each others' scents, which can trigger an enormous variety of emotional responses. Smell is one of our most primal senses, and it generates powerful feelings.

There's the tactile element. If you work in an office environment, or *any* environment that includes other people, you cannot avoid touching and being touched at least once in a while. Take, for instance, the common tactile ritual of shaking hands. What a peculiar custom! Who ever thought it up? Actually, handshaking may have originated centuries ago when knights would extend an open hand to show that they were not carrying concealed weapons and that they meant no harm. Metaphorically, shaking hands means more or less the same thing in the modern business world. Emotionally speaking, it means so much more. The grip of a hand, dry or wet, warm or cold, firm or soft, communicates a million subtle messages to our brains. Hands are arguably one of the most personal parts of the body; they're what we engage the world with and are our main organ of touch.

Tactile cues don't stop with handshakes, of course. There is the light tap on the arm, the accidental bump to the shoulder, the occasional knee pat. This is delicate stuff, and it's all very intimate, isn't it?

What You Hear . . .
and Don't Hear

Voices convey a universe of feeling, too. Even on the phone—and this includes voice-mail messages—the intonations in a person's voice will affect your perceptions about his attitude and impact your feelings. Amazingly, this phenomenon also carries over to e-mail. Don't you detect a "tone" in any given e-mail? As you read, you hear a little voice in your head, don't you? While you're reading an e-mail from a coworker or your boss, you "hear" her speaking the words that are before your eyes on the screen, and it calls forth all sorts of feelings and responses.

So how can you *not* take work personally, when it is so clearly a personal experience in every respect?

It's simple. Though all business is personal, it is not *about you.*

While people's words and behaviors affect you personally, they are *not a reflection on you*—they are merely an expression of people doing what they do, trying to get what they're trying to get, and being who *they* are.

You can detach yourself from much of the drama of your workplace if you can remember this simple distinction. The *experience* you're having is very personal. But other people's ways of conducting themselves in the workplace are *not about you*. Especially with difficult and challenging people, it's essential to keep this in mind.

Office cultures are a phenomenon unto themselves. People are going to be who they are, regardless of who you are. All of it affects you as a person, but you don't have to take it personally. Isn't that wonderful?

**Symptoms of a
"Diseased" Work
Environment**

- People gossip behind each other's backs.
- Interpersonal conflicts are never resolved.
- There's a feeling of tension and stress.
- People compete in cut-throat fashion.
- Employees are generally more worried about "looking good" than they are interested in accomplishing team goals.

- There is little or no sense of teamwork.
- Everyone is afraid of losing his or her job.
- For the most part, coworkers don't trust each other.

Treatments
- Be positive in putting forth solutions.
- Be honest in your dealings with coworkers.
- Be fair in evaluating yourself and others.
- Model trustworthy, professional, and discrete behavior.

4 the dysfunctional boss

Everybody's
Had One Managing relationships with supervisors, managers, and executives presents unique challenges. It is often easy to feel powerless with a small say in resource allocation, business strategy, and corporate policy. It would certainly level the playing field a great deal if subordinates had the power to fire their bosses, but unfortunately this will not be possible for most of us anytime soon.

Remember that at some point everybody is a boss, and everybody is a subordinate. You may think that a powerhouse like Bill Gates isn't accountable to anyone, but there are directors, bankers, and attorneys-general in different states, countries, and governments watching him. On some level, everyone participates in the give-and-take of authority.

It will likely come as no surprise that the most common reason people leave a job is conflict with the boss. Your relationship with your boss is tricky because by definition it is not a relationship of equals. Your boss has power to change things; you do not. It's not like your relationship with your coworkers; they are more or less on the same level with you and have the same recourse when there's a problem. As Michael Feiner states in *The Feiner Points of Leadership,* "Bosses set the ceiling on your career and they have all the electoral votes—they control pay, assignments, creature comforts, and access to senior people."

Understanding Your Boss

Knowing your boss's personality type will provide valuable insight into her strengths and weaknesses. Again in the words of Michael Feiner, "You need to *know your boss*. Who he or she is, what motivates him or her, what his or her priorities and goals are. . . . What are his hot buttons, fears, and ambitions? What makes her tick? What are his weaknesses? And of course, what are her expectations of you?"

You can make yourself indispensable to your boss by helping her shore up her weaknesses and capitalize on her strengths. After you have determined your boss's personality type, begin developing your customized relationship and communication system with her to enhance your performance and improve your effectiveness.

Types of Bosses

A number of years ago Worth Ethic, an executive coaching company, surveyed 1,500 business people and, from this, devised four categories of leaders. You probably could conduct a different survey and come up with other categories, but these four are as good a place to start as any. Always remember that no person fits exactly one category. He or she may fit *primarily* into a particular category, but there is plenty of overlap. Each type of leader has certain strengths, and each has a dark side, too. It's those dark sides that need to be managed.

The Commander

The Commander is energetic, decisive, and motivational. Jack Welch, CEO of General Electric, is a good example. But take these traits too far, and the same boss can be domineering, intimidating, uncontrollable, and even abusive.

THE HEALTHY COMMANDER

If you have a Commander for a boss, you might feel awed by her. She is so sharp, so talented, so sure of herself. She is the star of the show. Sometimes, her energetic,

A "Touchy" Boss

The BUSINESS
Shrink

Some people are more touchy feely than others. And different people interpret physical touch in different ways.

Suppose I get a call from Ben in Georgia, who gets annoyed every time his boss wants to shake his hand.

BEN: Why does he have to hold out his hand for me to shake every day? Okay, I know he likes me. He tells me I'm doing a good job. I get it. But what's with this handshake business all the time? I don't like to touch people a whole lot. But how can I tell my boss that? I don't know why he wants to shake my hand all the time, and I don't know how to tell him that I don't appreciate it. He's also got this horrible habit of slapping me on the back. I'd say he does that once or twice a day too.

Ben has got to take a chance in a situation like this, because if he can't tolerate the way he's being touched and can't get the boss to change it, he won't be able to stand going to work.

ME: Ben, you have to lay it on the line. Ask for a minute or two to talk to your boss privately. Then tell him very politely and respectfully that you're just not someone who likes to be touched all the time. Tell him you appreciate he's friendly, but you prefer not to shake hands every day, and the back slaps are a little startling. Tell him you appreciate that he's a good boss and that he gives you lots of encouragement, but you prefer verbal encouragement. Tell

him that's just the way you are. You don't have to apologize for it, and you don't have to be angry. But if he gets mad at you, or if he continues to expect handshakes and keeps slapping your back, you have every right to file a grievance at your company. Be sure to make a note of the conversation.

Sometimes the best approach to a problem is to confront it directly. After all, the boss probably couldn't read Ben's mind. Maybe some honest, direct communication could clear up the whole uncomfortable mess. Sure enough . . .

FOLLOW-UP: A MONTH LATER

A month later I get a call from Ben.

BEN: Well, I spoke to my boss, just like you said I should. And he was very understanding. He looked me in the eye, and he actually apologized. He said, "Sometimes I try too hard. It's not just about trying to make you feel encouraged. I guess it's also my unfortunate way of trying to be liked. So I appreciate your honesty with me about it. It took guts to come and tell me what you did. I won't be asking for handshakes or slapping you on the back anymore, I promise. Okay? Let's shake on it!" And then he laughed—he was only joking about "shaking on it." Thank goodness.

Honest and respectful communication is usually well received by people who are emotionally healthy. ∎

incisive style leaves you breathless with excitement. It's inspiring to work for such a super-confident leader. If she's an astute Commander, she can bring out the best in you and your coworkers. She will know how to use your talents in the most effective ways and give you a strong sense of your own potential.

THE
DYSFUNCTIONAL
COMMANDER

A powerful Commander who's callous and cold may frighten and humiliate her employees. Such leaders are dismissive of humanity and intolerant of foibles. This type of boss can slice you to bits with a harsh word or look that leaves you gasping for air. You may wind up scared to come to work; you may flinch when she walks by. The more intimidated you feel, the more cutting this boss becomes.

So first, collect yourself. Check in with your emotions, and give yourself acceptance and compassion. This is a tough situation—you have a dragon breathing fire down your neck. But your self-esteem does not depend on what this boss thinks of you or how she talks to you. Review your accomplishments, and keep in mind that you were a competent, worthwhile person before encountering this boss, and you're just as valuable today as you ever were. If this boss is unappreciative, then this is indicative of a weakness on her part, no matter how in command she seems.

DEALING WITH A
COMMANDER

Next, decide upon a rational strategy for dealing with the Commander. Use logic. What are her expectations and requirements? How can you get your job done and stay out of her way? You must learn to separate the content of her words from their emotional charge. Providing she gives you reasonable assignments to complete, you can do so while finding ways to disengage from her overbearing personality. Above all, respect yourself. If you exude a quiet self-respect, the Commander will sense it and respond favorably.

The Visionary   The visionary is epitomized by Steve Jobs of Apple. "Think different" was the company's slogan for a while, and it's presumably his personal slogan as well. At his best, the Visionary is creative, ambitious, and able to inspire others. This type may not be as adept at the nuts and bolts of managing, but he knows when to hire good people to run the show and how to get out of their way. The Visionary's dark side shows up when he doesn't get out of the way. The Visionary can err by trying to run everything himself, because he tends to be a bit impractical, not to mention unrealistic, which can make him over-confident. When challenged, he will become defensive rather than listening to other people's good ideas.

THE HEALTHY   A good Visionary boss will give you the opportunity
VISIONARY   to think outside the box along with him. In fact, a healthy, confident Visionary *encourages* his underlings to be imaginative and to play a role in creating the future of the team or company. Working for a Visionary can be exhilarating and can make life feel marvelous and magical. You may find yourself laughing at work more than you're used to. You may conceive newfound respect for the hitherto unsuspected brilliance of your coworkers. You may find yourself part of a wonderful, exciting, groundbreaking team project!

THE   On the other hand, things can get a little weird. Your
DYSFUNCTIONAL   inspirational leader's vision may be addled by delusions of
VISIONARY   grandeur. The imbalanced Visionary can be like a drunken ship's captain, unwilling to step away from the helm and let somebody else steer for a while, even though the vessel is veering toward the rocks and the whole voyage, not to mention the crew, is in danger. If you question his judgment, you may get shouted at or even fired. Worse yet, if the Visionary starts to feel paranoid or out of control, he'll start telling you how to do *your* job, which he most likely does not fully understand.

When you're working for a Visionary gone amuck, take the following steps:

1. Band together with your coworkers to discuss the situation.
2. Figure out feasible alternative directions for your department or team.
3. Approach the boss respectfully, as a delegation, and discuss the problem.

There is strength in numbers, and there's a chance that when he sees your views reflect much of the department's, your Visionary boss may listen to reason.

If your boss seems completely out of touch with the reality of your situation, consider getting together with colleagues and approaching his immediate supervisor or the Human Resources department. There are dangers to this approach, however. Strictly speaking, you are being insubordinate, violating the chain of command, and implicitly demonstrating disrespect for your boss. In a case like this, it is crucial that you document to your boss's superior what is going on. If you decide on this alternative, it may be best to work through the Human Resources department, which is responsible for dealing with conflicts between employees and their bosses.

The Strategist
The Strategist is intelligent, objective, highly analytical, and an adept problem solver. She's someone who is always thinking about what will happen five or ten years down the line. Alan Wurtzel, who inherited a small, debt-ridden electronics store from his father in 1973 and slowly built it into the Circuit City superstore empire, was a brilliant Strategist.

However, these leaders sometimes play their cards so close to their chest that they become secretive and smug. At worst, they turn into blatant manipulators. They become so preoccupied with moving people around like chess pieces in their private strategic game that they lose sight of the goal, forgetting that employees are people, not just pawns. Unless there are other humanizing forces in the company's management, Strategists are often doomed to fail in the long haul, no matter how productive they may appear at the outset.

THE HEALTHY STRATEGIST

Working for a Strategist who plays an open hand can be most edifying. You can learn a lot and get glimpses into the bigger picture of how your job fits into the company's overarching objectives. If you are lucky, your Strategist boss will also be a good communicator and will share her strategy with you, so that you can watch as it unfolds. You might not get to call the plays, but you can see how the pieces fit together, which is often gratifying. If you are thinking about going into business for yourself some day, the Strategist can be an outstanding mentor.

THE DYSFUNCTIONAL STRATEGIST

On the other hand, working for a Machiavellian Strategist can be a nightmare. One thing about this type of boss is that she treats all her employees equally—that is, with contempt. So long as you serve her purposes in some fashion, she'll keep you around and not bother you much. But if you're of no use to her, you may well be out the door in a heartbeat. Or she may just find a way to make your life miserable by trying to mold you into part of her mysterious plan, giving you orders and tasks that seem contradictory or confusing.

DEALING WITH A STRATEGIST

A manipulative Strategist is the most difficult type of boss. You don't have many options aside from supporting and being supported by your coworkers, as you all try to get by. In most cases, the manipulative Strategist will probably overreach herself eventually, overestimate her own power and charisma, and get herself fired. In the meantime, do what you can to protect yourself. Don't take the manipulative Strategist's actions or words

the pressure—then inflicting all of this on everybody else. You've probably worked for a Type A Boss at some point in your career.

Somehow you have to try not to "own" their crazy stress. Laugh about it in private with your coworkers. Keep reminding yourself that your work is not your whole life, and your boss is not a reliable reflection of your worth as an employee. Do your job and keep a low profile. Sooner or later, your boss will burn out; don't let him burn *you* out on the way.

Then there's Type B, the polar opposite of Type A. Type B bosses lack ambition and don't feel a driving sense of urgency or competitiveness about anything. Type Bs are more laid back, trusting, accepting, and patient than Type As, but they also tend to be more careless when it comes to taking care of things that really do need attention. They won't cause you a stress-induced heart attack, but their extremely easygoing nature brings a different set of problems, such as lack of focus and direction. A Type B boss may unintentionally stall your career by not providing you with challenges or goals that can enhance your image within the company.

With a Type B boss, you need to be assertive yet respectful. Call the boss's attention to work you're doing and projects that need to be completed. Ask the boss for meetings once a week or so, and prepare questions about the department's current goals and objectives and where your job fits in. Let the boss know that you are alert and on top of business, so that the boss will also feel prodded to step up to the plate.

Fortunately, these two "alphabet bosses" represent extremes. Most supervisors fall somewhere in the sane and balanced middle.

The Crusader Boss

There is the kind of boss I call Type C for "Crusader." A Crusader is someone who doesn't just command and control others but is constantly organizing and subordinating all activities to a particular agenda. This type of boss can really tear you up, because you feel guilty if you're not constantly overworking yourself and accepting substandard pay and working conditions for the good of the cause. Objecting makes you worse than insubordinate; it makes you a traitor. Organizations such as nonprofits and labor unions often attract Crusader bosses, but a Crusader can appear in any corporate environment.

The Crusader may be well intentioned, but he drains his people. His agenda may (or may not) be a noble one, but that's beside the point. His Great Purpose leaves no space for simple human needs.

DEALING WITH A CRUSADER BOSS
If you should fall under a Crusader's dominion, maintain a sense of proportion and scope. You have a life that is separate from your work, and you need to safeguard that. Your sense of meaning in life does not depend on your organization's mission, much less on your boss's blinkered agenda.

You face two unappealing choices: You can bear your boss's displeasure with your "lack of commitment," or you can burn yourself out. I recommend the first choice. It's far more livable. Most Crusaders are not vicious people; they will not fire you or deliberately find ways to make you miserable if you disappoint them. They *will* communicate their disapproval, and it won't be pleasant, but trying to meet their insane expectations is even less pleasant.

The Bully Boss
Unfortunately, bullying, abusive bosses are a very common breed. These bosses thoughtlessly wield their authority like a club to psychologically batter their employees. They may scream and yell. They may dump all their frustrations—both personal and professional—on you. They may call you names. They may tease you in a mean-spirited, even humiliating fashion. They toss about insults casually.

Because they're the boss, you can't shout back or ridicule them in turn without risk of losing your job. (Not that shouting and ridiculing are skillful means of resolving conflict, but it's irksome, to say the least, that you could be fired for the same type of behavior that your boss engages in habitually, with impunity.) And you can't exactly get away from your boss.

Though no one states this "policy" out loud, the common expectation is that you're supposed to simply allow bosses their "moods." The abusive boss may even offer half-hearted apologies once in a while and say something like "I know I came down a little hard on you yesterday. I'm sorry." He may give you a paternal pat on the back, which he imagines makes everything better. Bullying bosses are often convinced that a simple apology will wipe the slate clean, and their employees won't carry any residual bad feelings from an abusive episode. Since it's so easy to apologize and set things right when they have to, it's also no big deal to be abusive again, when the next bad day comes along. After all, you will understand—at least you'd better!

DEALING WITH A BULLY BOSS

If you have an abusive boss, what are your options? You can schedule a meeting and talk frankly with your boss about his behavior and how it affects you. If your boss is reasonably rational, he might understand when you say, "Look, next time you don't like a piece of work I've produced, could you please tell me privately, in a civil tone, instead of chewing me out in front of the entire office? I was really shaken up by the way you dressed me down publicly the other day. I know you were upset, but if you want me to do a better job, it would help if you treat me respectfully. After all, I work hard and I generally produce good work."

Or say: "I know you like to make jokes, and you don't mean any harm, but I'm sensitive, especially about my appearance. I'd really appreciate if you would stop making little quips and jibes about my weight. It's embarrassing and hurtful to me. In fact, I'd rather you didn't tease me about anything at all."

Some abusive bosses will hear you and shape up (although you might have to remind them once in a while), but others will chuckle and tell you to just "Get over yourself," or shoot back any number of other dismissive responses. It's very important that you document your meeting with the boss. You might want to follow it up with a memo to the boss repeating what you said and what he said. Establish a paper trail.

Assuming the meeting wasn't productive, next go to Human Resources to explain the problem and find out

66 99 | **Advice for managers: Avoid micromanaging.**

When delegating responsibility, afford your employees the authority necessary to fulfill the task at hand. Also, make sure they have the resources required to complete the job. Not to do so is a step on the road to micromanaging.

Micromanaging robs your employees of power and initiative. A smart manager avoids constantly peering over team members' shoulders.

An old friend in the television news business was working on an assignment with a new camera operator who had an excellent reputation for getting those special visual angles that make a reporter's story stand out from the competition. Part of this assignment was to capture the image of an unusual pinball machine. The reporter, who was used to dealing with less creative camera operators, said, "Please get me a shot in which your lens tracks the ball from moment of impact all the way through the maze." Immediately, the cameraman put his camera on the floor, turned to the reporter, and said, "Look, I know you're used to dealing with guys who just point and shoot, but they ain't me! Stay out of my head! Don't uncreate my job for me! This is what I live for!" The reporter got the message and figured out a better way to communicate.

So rather than micromanaging, find ways to empower your team members, and you'll see your bottom line increase.

what the company policy is on harassment and mistreatment. After familiarizing yourself with this information, you can file a formal grievance, though if you take this step you should have documentation and, preferably, witnesses to the alleged behavior.

If your company does not have a clear-cut formal grievance procedure, you might just have to steel yourself against your boss's insensitivity. Take some deep breaths, get up and leave the room, and go outside for an impromptu walk the next time the boss verbally beats up on you. If the boss's abuse isn't constant or isn't always directed at you personally, maybe you can simply accept it and deal with it on an episodic basis.

Then again, the danger with this approach is that one of your boss's assaults might just catch you when you're having a bad day of your own, and the temptation to explode or otherwise break down might be overwhelming. You may feel like you just need to stand up for yourself this once, and damn the torpedoes!

If you decide to confront your boss, do it in front of other employees, who can act as witnesses. First of all—and this may seem obvious but it bears mentioning—refrain from physical violence. Stand firm, look your boss in the eye, and state your limits. Tell your boss, in the way that comes naturally to you, that his behavior is intolerable and unacceptable, and you will not be treated this way. Do not use abusive language. You want to come across as a complete professional. If you're fortunate, your boss may be so stunned that he'll never bother you again.

The Absentee Boss   There is a lot of chatter about "leaderless" work environments and "peer supervision." This is all well and good, but if you're *supposed* to have a boss—that is, if there is a person who is explicitly designated as your supervisor, the person whom you supposedly report to and to whom you're responsible—then you want that person to *act like*

Pushing Back Against Abuse

The executive producer of a TV news department where a colleague once worked had an ugly habit of using his authority to bully people in a big, booming baritone voice. Everyone hated him for it. One day he bellowed across a crowded newsroom at a writer, declaring that she had royally screwed up a piece of work by rendering some data incorrectly. But he was mistaken, and the writer knew he was off base. Her instinct was screaming at her not to take the executive producer's abuse, and she listened to that inner voice. She yelled back, just as loudly as he had yelled at her, that her numbers were exactly on target and that his were wrong.

He thought about it for a moment, realized that she was right, and quietly mouthed an apology.

"Not good enough!" the writer shouted back. "I want you to apologize for criticizing me and say I was right at the same *sound level* you used for your false accusation!"

By now, the whole newsroom had fallen silent, transfixed, watching the battle. The bullying supervisor, who had never realized just how offensive his behavior had become, hesitated, smiled, and roared, for everyone to hear: "Attention everyone, I was *dead wrong* and she was correct! I should not have accused her of screwing up without making damn sure I was right! I was wrong, and I apologize!"

From that moment on, the climate of that office changed. It went from toxic to healthy. Thanks to the writer's courage and the boss's honesty, the quality of life improved for everyone who worked there.

Such beautiful happy endings may be rare. But at the very least, if you stand up for your convictions and do so in a dignified manner, your bullying boss just might be discouraged from abusing you again any time soon. ∎

a boss to some degree. I don't mean "boss you around" necessarily, but she should give guidance, set direction and goals, review your work, coordinate activity, and run the department.

But sometimes that person scarcely involves herself in the workflow and leaves it to you and other subordinates to guess what she wants and when she wants it. If you think this is a cushy situation, chances are you've never had a boss like this. A boss who doesn't lead is like a driver who doesn't steer. It's unsettling and very stressful. You don't know where you're going or who or what is going to meet you once you get there. For all you know, your ride could end with a pink slip or layoff—or some other sort of crash you can't imagine.

This nonmanaging manager is so laid-back and tolerant that she doesn't want to "lay a trip" on anyone, or provide any feedback about how they're doing. She also doesn't want to tell other people what to do, assuming that her staff pretty much knows what they're doing. Perhaps she fears offending them. (This is no joke! There are bosses who are afraid to assign tasks for fear of upset-

---

❝ ❞   Advice for managers: Watch yourself in action.

Many managers who consider themselves completely free of prejudice are actually guilty of discrimination. Without necessarily intending to, do you call upon, or take the advice of people of your own race or gender more often or more seriously than members of other ethnicities or the other gender? You might not even know or believe you're doing this, but others will notice. This behavior is damaging to workplace morale. Over time, those whose opinions you don't seek will feel that you have created a hostile work environment for them because their input and ideas are consistently dismissed. A hostile work environment is grounds for legal action under laws prohibiting workplace harassment.

Watch yourself in action, and be diligent about including and acknowledging all employees equally.

ting their underlings!) Or she has an excessive amount of respect for each individual's autonomy. She believes every person has his or her own unique "gift," and she wants to "stay out of the way" of each person's one-of-a-kind contribution to the organization and its mission. Precisely where you fit into that mission—or her department's mission for that matter—is not for her to define; she would not be so presumptuous as to assume she can determine your path for you.

Sounds empowering, doesn't it? It's exactly the opposite. It's chaos.

In an atmosphere such as this, strange and unpleasant things start to happen. Serious workers become frustrated that they're not getting any feedback and have no instrument or standard by which to measure the quality and efficiency of their work. People become a little loopy and paranoid. Some try to pretend that they're on the boss's wavelength and that they understand what's going on. Others become irritable or even competitive in odd ways. They half-consciously sense that eventually somebody is going to judge their performance, so for the time being they grasp at the only criterion that's available—comparing themselves to their coworkers.

Tensions build. Passive aggression becomes the norm rather than an aberration. The office becomes divided into two camps: those who are in denial that anything is wrong and are trying frantically to exude a calm attitude of enchanted engagement with the genius of the naturally unfolding workflow; and those who are furious at the boss for showing no leadership and feel contempt and disdain for their coworkers. Morale deteriorates, and the backbiting becomes vicious. No one feels connected to their jobs anymore.

DEALING WITH AN ABSENTEE BOSS

Nobody wants to say anything to the boss, however, because, first of all, she's really nice, and second, what's the use? She'll probably smile indulgently, validate your feelings, and ask you what *you* really need from a meaningful work environment.

At some point, though, someone has to step forward and provide a reality check, because that's the only way things will change. I recommend convincing the boss to have a meeting with you, and then try to persuade her that project accountability, including explicitly defined milestones, are her idea and that you are strongly committed to supporting her in those measures and goals.

Or ask for a group meeting with your boss and a coworker who sees things the way you do. In that meeting, be frank with your boss about what you see going on. Let her know that the lack of structure and direction, far from empowering her workers, is actually detrimental to the culture and productivity of the workplace. Offer suggestions for what she might do differently. Give her a list of actions you would appreciate seeing her take, such as setting periodic productivity goals, holding regular staff meetings (for which she, as boss, would set the agenda), and noticing and rewarding outstanding work performance. Be clear that you are very unhappy and anxious about the way things at the office are (not) being run and that you are not alone in your feelings.

Perhaps your overly mellow boss will get the message and begin stepping up to her responsibilities a little more. If not, keep trying. Keep organizing your colleagues and approaching her. You want your boss to do her job, just as you'd expect she wants you to perform yours.

The Half-Time Boss   Some bosses think, incorrectly, that one of the perks of being a boss is that no one watches you. Naturally, some of them take advantage of this. They come in a bit later than everyone else, take longer lunches, and leave an hour earlier.

Why is this a problem? Well, for one thing, it's not fair. Why should you have to work a full day and brave rush-hour traffic or a crowded commuter train each morning to get to the office by 8:30 when your boss nonchalantly waltzes in at 10:00? Why is it necessary for you to be "on the clock," while your boss is apparently more "project-oriented" about his time commitment to the job?

Even if your boss is generally effective and fair in every other way, his short hours are going to be noticed—and probably resented—by the people who work under him. Whether he realizes it or not, he is sending a confusing message to his workers. Either his casual attitude about working hours means, "There is a different standard in effect here for me than there is for you," or "Work hours and timeliness really aren't that big a deal in this office and should not be taken too seriously."

If you perceive the first message, you are likely to feel indignant and insulted. If you perceive the second, you might start taking flex hours yourself. So might the rest of the office. Then problems arise when people start coming in at different times, and nobody understands exactly when they're supposed to be at work or when they're supposed to take lunch. The next thing you know, you can't find the person who has the information you need to finish a task or project.

To be fair, the Half-Time Boss may have reasons for being late or leaving early. He may have a chronically sick child or an invalid parent who requires his attention, or he may put in many hours of work at home. But if he doesn't communicate any of this to his staff, he leaves them free to make the worst assumptions about his cavalier attendance patterns. Even if he has a good reason for not keeping regular hours, he is nonetheless exercising a *privilege* that the rest of the office is not permitted to enjoy.

DEALING WITH A HALF-TIME BOSS

His short hours do not always create a big problem. People can ignore it, or they can find ways to appreciate the boss for what he does right and motivate each other to stay committed to the work at hand.

But if the situation has a negative effect on team morale, someone needs to communicate it to the boss. He may not realize that his short hours are a problem. Someone should respectfully encourage him to address the issue with the whole team. It might even be a good topic to discuss during a staff meeting. Perhaps you and a coworker could approach him and delicately make the suggestion.

The Idea Stealer

Some bosses assume that every original idea or successful accomplishment that comes out of their department is their private property. Rather than bestowing praise and prestige on their staff, they hoard the glory for themselves. They imply that *they* had the great idea or *they* closed the sale or *they* got the project finished ahead of deadline—or at least they had a critical hand in it.

This behavior can be demoralizing and have other consequences. The credit-mongering boss may receive promotions she doesn't deserve, while the hardworking team members receive no accolades, much less a raise.

DEALING WITH AN
IDEA STEALER

If you have a boss who routinely fails to award appropriate credit, you might consider getting the issue out on the table. But be strategic about it. Think of your boss's personality. Is she likely to listen to you? Or will she react defensively even if you are respectful and clear in your presentation of the problem? Should you approach her alone, or with coworkers who feel the same way? You don't want her to feel as if you're ganged up on her, but then again, it might be more convincing from two or three people rather than just one. After all, she may not even realize what she has been doing.

Based on your overall judgment of the boss's character, if you think that she may be receptive to your concerns, it's important to have on hand recent specific examples of achievements for which you and your fellow workers did not receive proper credit. Otherwise, she may not understand what you're talking about. It may be obvious to you and your colleagues, but people often have a blind spot when it comes to their own dark side. (Maybe that's why it's called a *dark* side.) If you present easily recalled instances—"You know, when I worked overtime four nights in a row to finish that report, and at the general staff meeting you just said that 'we' should be proud that 'we' did it."—then your boss may open her eyes a little wider and say, "Ah, I see what you mean. I *should* have given you credit. I'm so sorry."

It is best not to frame your dissatisfaction as a general complaint against her character. Speak of your experiences and your desire to be recognized for what you do. Never bring up examples about others who are not present. That will only muddy the waters and possibly create distrust toward your unwitting coworker.

If, despite your conversation, the boss continues to (deliberately or unconsciously) neglect to give you appropriate credit and recognition for your best achievements, then you need to figure out other ways of making those achievements more noticeable to your coworkers and to other persons in your organization. Don't depend on your boss to publicize your great work. Talk about your latest project and your creative ideas with lots of people. Say, "You know, I'm so glad I had that idea for the new procedure. I think everyone is happier now that the work flows so much faster and smoother around here." The other person might ask, "You mean, *you* thought of it?" And you say, "Yes, of course it was me. You mean you didn't know?" Be careful not to appear boastful, and always remember to give credit to those who worked on ideas that you originated, including your boss if she did.

The Personal Affront

A more delicate situation occurs when an abusive boss chooses you, and only you, to be his personal whipping boy or girl. For some inexplicable reason, your boss has

Regular performance appraisals are critical for morale and for keeping both the business and its employees functioning at peak performance levels. Some experts think evaluations should be held once a year; others say twice. But frequency is not as important as the consistency and integrity of the process.

Employees need feedback, encouragement, and the opportunity to improve. On my radio show I asked Sharon Armstrong, a human resources consultant for more than twenty years, to explain the seemingly oxymoronic title of her book *Stress-free Performance Appraisals*. She said, "It can be stress-free if you follow some simple techniques."

What you want to avoid, according to Armstrong, are common mistakes, such as:

- Favoritism—Overlooking the flaws of favorite employees.

- Grouping—Excusing below-standard performance because "everyone does it."

- The Halo/Horns Effect—Letting one particular behavior you like or dislike dictate your entire opinion of an employee, overlooking other factors.

- Overly Time-Sensitive Evaluation—Allowing some recent behavior or event to obscure your view of everything that your employee has done during the rest of the entire evaluation period.

You should be keeping track of employee performance continuously. Waiting until the last minute to think about an evaluation means you'll have to base your review on the most unreliable instrument of all—your memory. When an employee's review time approaches, start thinking about it at least one month ahead of time so that your thoughts can gel and you can develop some perspective.

It's part of the manager's job to create a proper, cordial environment for the evaluation meeting and to make sure there are no surprises for the employee. Spring an unpleasant surprise on an employee during a review, Armstrong says, and he or she may respond in a way you don't expect. You can avoid this if you've been doing your job all along: setting clear goals and expectations, and keeping lines of communication open throughout the year.

taken a particular and intense dislike to you, and he takes every opportunity to let you know it. He may harass you with extra and unreasonable tasks, single you out for excessive criticism at staff meetings, belittle your efforts and ideas, and even give you a spiteful, unfair employee evaluation.

This is an extremely tough situation. As always in these situations, document everything. If matters are extreme, go to Human Resources and discuss the matter with them. You may also consider contacting an attorney; after all, this situation may represent harassment, which is not only unethical but illegal. But if you do, the HR representative or attorney is going to want a lot of detailed evidence.

If you decide not to go to HR, maybe you can grit your teeth and tough it out until your boss gets tired of bothering you and goes after someone else instead or simply goes away. Maybe he's taking out his frustration on you because he actually hates his job, or his home life is falling apart, or—who knows? Maybe you remind him of somebody he disliked or who injured him in some way. Unfortunately, there is no way for you to know or to address this sort of thing.

Then again, he may be picking on you because you are very competent and do an excellent job. Some bosses feel threatened by that; they're afraid you might be smarter than they are (and they might be right).

Above all, don't let this boss pressure you into quitting or into doing something really stupid, like losing your cool. Don't give him an obvious excuse to go after you. In most midsize to large companies, your boss will have to document his reasons for firing you. If there is no justification, you could have a strong case for a grievance, especially if you're a member of a union and your coworkers have witnessed the personal abuse you've suffered.

Of course, you also have the option to quit. Your decision will naturally depend on how attached you are to your current position. Is it time for a change anyway? Or were you hoping to retire from this job? If you're unsure whether you can afford to look for another job at this point in your career, make a list of the benefits, costs, and risks of staying versus going.

Preparing for Performance Evaluations with Your Boss

Perhaps the most critical (and sometimes stressful!) feedback mechanism you have at work is your periodic performance appraisal or review, which is generally delivered by your boss.

Some companies have adopted an employee-driven approach to performance reviews, which managers love because it takes much of the burden off them. The employee starts the process, brings her goals and results together, gets input about her performance from other people she's worked with, and fills out a self-assessment. Only then is it time for a meeting with the boss and a discussion that's based (theoretically) on a calm, thorough, factual evaluation.

Regardless of the process, remember to document your performance and accomplishments, even if it's as simple as keeping an ongoing list in a folder at the front of your file cabinet. This is the professional thing to do in order to make sure your accomplishments are remembered at review time. Your boss may even appreciate the reminders. Then if there is any disagreement, you have documentation to back up your case.

If you have a good relationship with your boss and have consistently given your best effort on the job, your performance review is unlikely to contain any unpleasant surprises. However, if your boss has been lackadaisical about tracking your performance or is unfair or simply unskilled at providing a thorough and balanced employee evaluation, your experience of being evaluated may turn out to be disappointing or upsetting.

If you find yourself blindsided by an unfavorable report, which will go on record in your personnel file, take the time and effort to compose a pointed, thorough, carefully written rebuttal to any points in the review that you feel are unjust. If your evaluation fails to give you sufficient credit for your achievements, write down what you think is missing from the report. You might not convince your boss that he or she has misperceived you, but at least your version of details and events will be on file, usually stapled to the boss's completed appraisal form. In many organizations, you are given a formal opportunity to comment on your performance review before signing off that you've read it and spoken about it with your boss. So take advantage of this chance to advocate for yourself, particularly if you have supporting documentation for your claims. It may favorably affect your future career opportunities, particularly within your company.

A Final Word about the Boss

Whatever type of boss you may have, remember that she is a human being who has limitations, just as you do. You usually cannot change your boss's behavior patterns, but you can navigate through them, minimize any negativity, and take care of your own emotions. You don't have to be constantly at the mercy of her emotional weather.

Try to understand where your boss is coming from, what interests she is protecting, what her fears and aspirations are, what troubles her, and what pleases or impresses her. In other words, get to know your boss and *manage* her. This is not manipulation. It is survival strategy and good business sense.

You can learn to recognize the different types of bosses and use these categories to help you understand the people you work for. But what matters most is how well you use your intelligence, maintain your self-respect, and bring integrity to your relationship with your boss.

**Symptoms of a
Dysfunctional
Boss**

- She screams a lot and speaks abusively.
- He consistently scapegoats a particular person or certain people.
- She isn't there half the time.
- He tries to micromanage everything his employees do.
- She takes undue credit for team members' ideas.
- He has grand visions and ideas but not a firm grasp on reality.
- She drives her employees to exhaustion and has unrealistic expectations of them.
- He is smug and manipulative.
- She is highly competitive and frantically overscheduled.
- He is overly laid-back, and seems scarcely interested in the mission of the workplace.

Treatments

- Communicate. Tell your boss what behavior is bothering you.
- Make alliances with your coworkers. Maybe you're not the only one upset about the boss's behavior.
- Document everything. If you have to escalate the situation, you'll need proof.
- Keep your cool. Losing your temper in front of everyone won't help.

5 handling dysfunctional boss behaviors

Working under Dysfunctional Circumstances

In the last chapter we looked at some extremely difficult bosses. Unfortunately, it's not only the blatantly bad bosses who can give you trouble. Any boss can exhibit a range of unpleasant behaviors that can make your life miserable once in a while or all the time. They say power corrupts, and it's true. Your boss may have the best of intentions and be basically a good person, but she wears a mantle of authority that can blind her when she's a bit thoughtless, arrogant, or even nasty.

It isn't easy working for someone. If your boss is consistently fair, considerate, decent, and humble, you are very lucky. Nearly everyone has to put up with offensive boss behaviors from time to time.

When the Boss Plays Favorites

Some bosses like one or two of their employees better than others, and they have ways of showing it. Sometimes this situation is merely annoying, and at other times, it can have serious consequences.

The boss may give his favorite the best assignments or even a promotion that somebody else deserves more. A boss can help his favorite look good by providing overly flattering performance evaluations or looking the other way when her performance is not up to par. The boss may blame other employees for his favorite's mistakes or shortcomings. He may be more likely to award his favorite a raise, let her take more days off, or give her the best office space or desk.

Even if the boss shows favoritism in less obvious ways, the result is a demoralized work force and resentment. If the boss defers to a particular employee during meetings, always seeking out this person's opinion to the exclusion of others, the rest of the group feels (correctly) that their input is not valued and they need not apply their minds to the task at hand. If their thoughts and ideas are not solicited, employees feel less invested in any given project.

A Lunchtime Clique   If the boss simply clearly prefers to "hang out" with one or two employees more than others at lunch or during casual moments throughout the day, this can create an implicit hierarchy in the workplace, with those "closer" to the boss occupying a higher rung on the social ladder. A certain amount of hierarchy is necessary for most organizations, but when the social hierarchy—defined by whom the boss views with favor—becomes an unstated pecking order that has little to do with seniority or job description, a corrosive oppression sets in.

Though it's a tough balancing act, the boss *should* treat all employees with equal regard, offering praise or constructive criticism *based entirely and exclusively on job performance.*

If you have a boss who plays favorites, and you are not among them, you probably feel angry, resentful, and even hurt. It is hard not to take his behavior personally. There is something innately threatening and painful about having the person you depend on, the person who has a certain amount of control over your fate, not appreciate you as a person.

So first, look at your feelings and try not to take his behavior to heart. It isn't your fault that the boss is being a jerk. No matter where you work or what the situation is, if your boss plays favorites, this is definitely *not* your fault, and your boss *is* being a jerk. That much is clear.

But even if you understand it's not your fault, how do you mitigate the practical consequences of favoritism? There are a number of ways to respond proactively. If it seems that your boss is going to promote his favorite ahead of you or give his favorite the project or contract that you should have, you have several options, depending on your office.

Dealing with Favoritism   The first option—and sometimes this really works!—is to lay it on the line. In a private meeting with your boss, respectfully but firmly point out how long you have been with the company, what impressive accomplishments you have achieved (be ready to modestly itemize them), and why you ought to receive a particular promotion or responsibility for a major project. You hope that the boss sees this and keeps you in mind, because this is your job and your career after all. If your boss is essentially fair-minded and you believe you can reason with her, this could be the best approach to take.

Then again, if your boss plays favorites so brazenly that an appeal to her reasonable side seems senseless and unsafe, consider talking to your office mates about the situation. Do they agree that the project or promotion should be yours? If so, there may be ways of leveraging their support—especially if they know they can count on you in similar circumstances. In an environment where the boss treats her employees unequally, it helps if the disfavored contingent band together in the event of conspicuous bias and unfair treatment. If you have allies, you can petition the boss together, either in a special meeting or at staff meeting. You can also go to the boss's supervisor or to Human Resources. As always, get the facts down on paper. Perhaps you won't have to file a grievance—that can poison your relationship with your boss permanently—but you never know when or in what way it may serve you to have documentation.

If the stakes are not quite so high, you can take a less confrontational approach. For example, if the boss defers to a particular person most of the time at meetings or

The Boss's Pet

Janet has worked as an English teacher at the local community college for nine years. Her student evaluations have been consistently strong, and she has taught a wide variety of basic and advanced courses. She is widely respected by her peers and by the district administration.

Evelyn has also worked in the district for nine years and has a resume similar to Janet's. Evelyn also enjoys a close and convivial relationship with the head of the English department; they go out to lunch together three or four times a week.

For three semesters in a row, Janet and Evelyn have both taught English 101, the main freshman English course. Janet has requested an evening teaching slot each semester, but the department head has consistently awarded that slot to Evelyn.

A week before the new fall semester begins, Janet gets her classroom assignment, and again, she is given daytime hours for all her classes. Janet pays a visit to her supervisor, Beatrice, the head of the English department.

Beatrice explains to Janet that the evening slot is Evelyn's because "it's always been Evelyn's."

"You mean it's been Evelyn's for the last three semesters," corrects Janet.

"Well," says Beatrice, shrugging. "I think that constitutes a precedent. I'm sorry. It's not fair to Evelyn for me to change her assignment now."

"I've been working here just as long as Evelyn, and I've requested that slot every semester, Beatrice."

Beatrice raises an eyebrow. "I don't think there's anything further to discuss, Janet. If you don't like your assignment, you can always apply to another district, where they might have need for someone who's only willing to teach in the evening."

"That's not fair, Beatrice!"

"I'm sorry, Janet. This conversation is over."

Frustrated and upset, Janet consults Kathy, another English teacher. "I'm going to file a complaint with the district," says Janet.

"You know who you should talk to first?" says Kathy. "Call Evelyn. She may not even know what's going on. Give her the benefit of the doubt. Beatrice is a jerk, but my experience is that Evelyn's a nice person. I don't know her that well, but she seems level-headed and if I were you, I'd speak with her before going to the district."

So Janet bites the bullet and calls Evelyn, the woman she's come to think of as her "opponent." They've only exchanged a few words in the past at department meetings, and Janet has perceived Evelyn as distant and aloof. But to Janet's surprise, Evelyn's voice on the phone is warm, and she seems genuinely appreciative that Janet has trusted her enough to call.

"Wow," says Evelyn. "So this has been bothering you for years! I had no idea!"

"Well," says Janet, "I wouldn't say 'years,' but definitely the last year and a half."

"Still," says Evelyn. "You're right. It isn't fair. I had no idea I was putting you out. I thought I was the only one who liked teaching in the evenings. All of our English teachers are women, and a lot of them feel unsafe walking to their cars after class in the dark."

"Doesn't bother me," says Janet. "I would feel safe. Or I could ask a student to escort me."

"Yeah, I've never had a problem," says Evelyn. "Tell you what. I'll drop an e-mail to Beatrice and just say that if she doesn't mind, if it's at all possible, I'd prefer to work days this semester. I'll tell her I spoke with you about it and you offered to switch class times with me."

"Are you sure she won't feel manipulated?" worries Janet aloud.

"I think *she's* the one who's been manipulative!" declares Evelyn. "I'm really sorry for how she talked to you. Don't worry. We'll work it out."

The moral of the story is, give the "boss's pet" a break until you find out where he or she is really coming from! You never know; the pet might be an ally, too. ■

chooses one or two "special" people with whom to be socially friendly, there are softer ways to counteract the ill effects of these behaviors. If your thoughts and ideas don't receive enough air time at staff meetings, prepare a memo before meetings about issues and suggestions that you'd like to see discussed. The boss is not likely to complain about this type of proactive preparation and forethought, especially if you present your memos in a respectful, professional manner. You can even be a bit bold, stepping in once in a while with a polite "Excuse me, I think Joan was about to make an interesting point a moment ago."

If the boss excludes you from the sunshine of her social attention in the office, there is not much you can do to change that, but why would you want to? So long as she shows no favoritism toward her friends, it actually makes life a bit simpler to have *less* rather than *more* casual interaction with the boss. Think about it. If your boss is also your "friend," you have to walk a line between deference and ease, between openness and circumspection. You don't need that type of relationship in your life! Let the boss's inner circle enjoy their little clique, while you enjoy the integrity of your work and your working relationships with colleagues.

What If the Boss   Then again, maybe *you* are the boss's favorite or one
Favors You?   of the chosen few. If so, it is incumbent on you to make sure that the boss does not award you special favors that disadvantage your colleagues. You have to be vigilant, you have to be diplomatic, and you have to exercise the utmost integrity. It is fine if you like your boss and it's even okay if you relate better to him than to most of the other people in your office, but it's a big problem if this relationship turns into a political football at work. Don't count on the boss to keep appropriate boundaries. *You* have to be careful not to take advantage of his favoritism.

Your office mates can see that you have special standing, and some (at least) are bound to resent it. Protect yourself by maintaining these relationships, too. Make a habit of showing respect and consideration and friendliness to your office equals, so that they trust you, feel at ease with you, and perceive you as one of them.

One danger is that your coworkers may bring their issues or problems with the boss to you first, which puts you in a precarious position. Always downplay your connection with the boss in these situations. You can say, "Well, I don't know. You might try asking him or saying that at the next meeting. I think you have a good point. Hopefully, he will hear that. I would certainly support your position at staff meeting." But never, *never* offer—or accept a request—to be somebody's ambassador. You are not a mediator or an advocate. That's not part of your job description. Don't be tempted into it, even for your best office friend.

Placing yourself in the middle of other people's conflicts or communication difficulties is a surefire way to get into trouble.

When the Boss Uses Harsh or Thoughtless Language

Sometimes bosses get cranky and say things that rankle. They may make an overly critical statement about your work, speak in an angry or condescending tone, or come down a little too hard. They may even make an unflattering comment about your clothes or an unkind joke at your expense, perhaps without meaning to hurt but leaving you upset and embarrassed all the same.

Unfortunately, you can't say to your boss, "Hey, I don't like your attitude in this conversation. Let's talk some other time." You also cannot snarl or make a demeaning joke without imperiling your standing.

What you can do is stand up for yourself respectfully. You could say, "I'm sorry you weren't pleased with my work. I'll revise it per your directions. But there's no need to snap at me. I understand you're frustrated, but I'm only human, and I'm doing the best I can, so please speak to me respectfully, and I'll keep trying to improve."

Or: "You know, I understand you're trying to be funny, but I didn't appreciate that joke. I found it a little insulting. I'd like to ask you please not to aim your humor at me anymore, all right?"

Look him in the eye and maintain a steady, calm tone. You have a right to be treated with respect. Some bosses lose it once in a while, but a normal boss may even apologize if you call him on an occasional lapse of manners. Your office mates will respect you more, too, if they see you standing up for yourself in a dignified, assertive (but not aggressive) way. In a sense, you're doing it for everyone, since the boss probably lets loose on other people too once in a while. The key is to give your boss plenty of "space" to save face. Don't make him apologize. Don't accuse. Simply state how *you* feel, and let the boss decide how to handle it. Some bosses won't say much; they'll just mumble something ambiguous and walk away. But they might be less likely to do it again.

If the boss responds with hostility to a humble, quiet statement such as the ones suggested, then you may have yourself a real problem boss. Refer to Chapter 4 for suggestions about how to handle raging, chronically abusive bosses.

When the Boss's Moods Are Unpredictable

One way bosses get careless is by letting their moods infect the workplace. When your boss is happy, why, the whole office is expected to be cheerful! It's a lovely day! But when the boss is grumpy, everybody watch out! Don't laugh, smile, and pretend that life is fine. Why should you be in good spirits if your boss isn't?

Many bosses don't realize that they expect the mood of the office to conform to their own. Even so, most bosses are on a fairly even keel, and they don't usually surprise you very much with the attitude they bring to work on any given day. Some bosses, however, have moods that shift like the weather. They may be jovial in the morning, edgy and irritable in the afternoon, and full of gossip as evening approaches. But you never know, because their patterns are always changing. The only thing you can be sure of is that the boss's moods are *strong*. So how do you insulate yourself against this type of "mood tyranny" in the workplace?

First, be clear about your own psychological boundaries. It's very important that you understand *consciously* that the boss's frame of mind is *separate from yours* and you do not *depend* on the boss for permission to feel good or to have your own moods, quite apart from anything the boss may be feeling. Say, the boss is cracking jokes, but you are preoccupied by your kid's problems at school. Well, guess what? You're not obligated to appreciate the boss's humor, and you don't have to laugh. Or the boss may have had a bad night's sleep or a fight with her husband the night before, so she comes in full of cynicism and ire about anything and everything, whereas you may have just enjoyed a lovely visit with an old college friend, and you're looking forward to a great weekend. It's okay to feel good even if the boss is feeling bad. It seems obvious, but it's easy to forget if your boss has an overbearing "moody" personality.

Finally, when the boss is in an evil temper, just stay out of her way. You don't have to be in the line of fire. When the boss is in a comedic mood but you're not, the same principle applies. Just keep your distance.

When the Boss Is Unresponsive to Your Needs

Sometimes you might have pressing needs at work, and the boss just isn't interested, or refuses to believe your needs are important. Perhaps you've been working too long and too hard and you need some time off. The boss thinks that's silly; she's been working just as long and hard as you have, and *she* doesn't need a break! Or you require more time to complete a project, and your boss does not understand, because she has a set idea of how long the project should take, and she doesn't understand the obstacles and challenges you need to overcome to finish

Crude Humor

C Suppose Georgette, a listener, calls me and says, "My boss has the most disgusting sense of humor on Earth. I don't think he means to offend, but he is always making crude and disgusting jokes."

ME: You mean, especially toward women?

GEORGETTE: No, no, it's not like that. He's not a sexual harasser. He's just a dork, and he likes a lot of bathroom humor. It's like . . . he's a little developmentally stuck or something.

ME: Have other people complained?

GEORGETTE: Well, not directly to him. He can be very sensitive, and a little reactive. It isn't safe to criticize him or offer "constructive feedback." He's not a bad person, but he's extremely immature.

ME: Well, can't you just ignore his humor?

GEORGETTE: I could try. But it definitely degrades the quality of life around the office. He tells gross jokes and makes crude allusions to bodily functions all the time, which seem to fascinate him. It sets a certain tone.

ME: I think I'm getting it. But listen—do you like jokes?

GEORGETTE: Do I like them? Well, if they're funny, sure. But his aren't funny.

ME: Can you think of any jokes that you like?

GEORGETTE: I know a few. I don't see where this is going though.

ME: Humor me. No pun intended. Tell me a joke.

GEORGETTE: Okay. Knock knock.

ME: Who's there?

GEORGETTE: Control freak.

ME: Control fr—

GEORGETTE (CUTTING ME OFF): Now *you* say "Control freak who!"

ME (LAUGHING): Why don't you try that joke on your boss?

GEORGETTE: Why?

ME: Next time he tells you a joke, or tells a joke when you're around, say, "Hey, I've got one for you." Try to remember some good, funny jokes that aren't disgusting. Maybe it'll gradually help him realize, in a gentle way, that there are lots of different ways to be funny and witty, and he doesn't always have to "push the edge" by being gross. It may not work, but it's a thought. And maybe your office mates will reinforce what you're doing. There's really no good reason that you all have to be affected by your boss's childish humor.

A sense of humor is a very personal thing. What's funny to some people is silly or disgusting to others. And sometimes a coworker or boss just needs a little nudge to tell him that he's being inappropriate.

Humor can also be a great way to defuse tension in the workplace, and that's what happened here.

FOLLOW-UP: A MONTH LATER

When Georgette calls back some time later, she reports, "My 'clean' jokes had an odd effect on the boss."

ME: Tell me.

GEORGETTE: Well, he hasn't laughed at a single one, though I think a few of them were pretty darn funny if I do say so myself.

ME: I'm sure they were. Your knock-knock joke knocked me out.

GEORGETTE: Ugh. I hate puns. Anyway, I got into the habit of telling him clean jokes, and at first he just responded by seeming uncertain how to respond. He looked puzzled. Not upset or offended or anything like that, but just . . . confused. And then just yesterday, he actually came up to me of his own accord and said, "You're not crazy about my jokes, are you?"

ME: You're kidding? Just like that?

GEORGETTE: Just like that. He didn't seem mad. He seemed . . . bemused. And he said, "You know, I admire your attitude. You only tell jokes that are clever. I tell jokes just to shock myself awake."

ME: Is that what he really *said*?

I was incredulous. These did not sound like the words of the "immature" man that Georgette had originally described.

GEORGETTE: Yeah and it was a very strange thing to say, because he certainly doesn't seem sleepy to any of the rest of us. Maybe he meant it in his own private way, I don't know. But anyway, I felt good about the conversation. It didn't go much beyond what I just told you, but it was a kind of sweet moment. And he's really toned down his office humor, or at least around me he certainly has.

ME: Well, how about that? You just never know with people. ∎

the task. Maybe there is a problem with your working environment: You need less noise, better lighting, more distance from an annoying coworker, a better ergonomic setup at your computer. But the boss pays no attention to such things. She's got more important things to worry

66 99   Advice for managers: Be aware of the perils.

Many a good worker has left a job that she otherwise liked, where she was doing fulfilling work or advancing her career, because of an insensitive or irresponsible supervisor. In many cases, the boss wound up losing an effective team member (or someone who could have been a valuable team member) because he failed to practice effective leadership. Losing a good employee is very expensive to a company. It squanders not only all of the resources invested in the training process but also a valuable team member who might now join the competition.

Always be mindful that your management, good or bad, can affect people for a long time in fundamental, career-altering ways. Of course, it shapes your future as well.

Once, a district manager for a New York City–based company repeatedly abused her power with employees, humiliating them and threatening their jobs. Unbeknownst to her, several of the employees began collecting her nasty memos and keeping meticulous notes on every hostile utterance and demeaning remark she made. These employees decided to appeal in writing to the president of the company. The president summoned the district manager to the company's home office and confronted her with the memos and the contemporaneous notes. She received three months' severance and medical benefits on the condition that she never return to the company.

In their book, *Values-Driven Business,* Ben Cohen and Mal Warwick explain succinctly what you need to remember about your workers: "What employees want (and need) the most is to be treated with dignity and respect as intelligent human beings capable of making their own contributions to the success of the company." When they are so treated, their talents and abilities will shine through in the workplace—and make *you* look good, too.

about than your niggling needs, and she sloughs off your concerns.

If your boss won't help you get what you need, you have to find other ways of getting your needs met. Get a doctor's order for that vacation time. Document the tasks involved in the project you're doing, and assign an estimated time requirement for each element of the project so that your boss can see it's more complicated than she thinks. Ask your coworkers politely to be quiet, bring an extra desk lamp to work, tell the annoying coworker to leave you alone and stop distracting you, find a better desk chair somewhere in the office or order one through the appropriate department.

But what if something you need really requires the boss's cooperation? What if you cannot get a particular need met without her help, and she is still not paying attention?

Then you need to make your case persistently, clearly, and assertively until she "gets it." Bring it up when you see her in the hall, send her an e-mail memo and copy relevant individuals, mention it at staff meeting, let others in the office know that you're having a serious problem. The boss won't be able to ignore you forever if you have a legitimate and imperative need, and you don't let her apathy demoralize you. Always be respectful of course, but don't allow yourself to be shunted aside when something really matters. You are as entitled to get your needs met as the next person (including the boss), and any reasonable boss will have to concede that sooner or later.

If the boss still categorically refuses to recognize your needs, then she is profoundly dysfunctional. See Chapter 4's section on "The Personal Affront."

When the Boss Is a Poor Communicator

Not all people know how to say what they mean, particularly if it is complicated or sensitive. Many bosses have communication difficulties. Some are simply inarticulate. Others are lazy and assume they don't have to explain things because their team members should know every-thing already. These types of bosses often seem to assume that their underlings should be able to read their minds. Then there are super-nice bosses, who hate to hurt any-one's feelings and are hesitant to give constructive criti-cism or to point out when something is not being done the right way.

The key is to get to know your boss and understand his ways of communicating. If he's of the super-nice vari-ety, you have to be attentive for indirect clues that he's not entirely satisfied with your performance. Then you have to gently inquire further and get him to explain what he wants and what he perceives. Or, if your boss is of the "you should read my mind" variety, try putting a lot of things in writing (e-mail is sufficient) and asking to receive information in writing whenever possible. If this boss gives you an assignment to do and you have a sneaking suspicion that he is also expecting more than he cares to specify, paraphrase what you've heard and ask, "Is that all?"

If your boss is simply unskilled at speaking in under-standable complete sentences, that's something you just have to get used to. Don't be afraid to ask for clarification. You won't be the only one in the office who needs it. One way or another, you have to find a means of adapt-ing to your boss's communication style.

When the Boss Hangs You Out to Dry

Sometimes a boss will assign you a complex task or project without providing you the information or resources you need to do it right. Even if you apply your-self diligently, your work ends up being insufficient, you look bad and feel even worse. Although you take respon-sibility, in truth it's your boss's fault because she failed to set you up properly. The boss has hung you out to dry.

The first step in avoiding or extricating yourself from such a predicament is to recognize when it's about to hap-pen. Take stock of what you need to complete any project,

achievements—such as a simple Excel chart illustrating your productivity or a binder of completed reports. Have them ready to show her to underscore your points as you speak. Be honest. Let her know that you are starting to feel worried that her lack of recognition could have practical implications for you down the line and you'd appreciate some reassurance that your talents and accomplishments are duly noted.

You might say, "I don't want you to feel as though you need to compliment me every day, but it's helpful to me if you can drop me a congratulatory e-mail when I finish a big project. It lets me know you're satisfied with my work." In the end, of course, be sure to thank your boss for meeting with you.

When the Boss Is Dishonest

Once in a while the boss does something less than honorable or tells a fib. He may not be a pathological liar, but he might play a little loose with the facts.

What effect does this behavior have on you and your department? If its impact is negligible, you can ignore it, reminding yourself not to take everything your boss says at face value.

Then again, if your boss tells a lie that compromises the integrity of the department, you might need to take action. Depending on the situation, it can be tricky.

If the boss asks *you* to do something dishonest—for example, exaggerate the profits generated by a particular sales campaign in a report to upper management—you have no choice but to respectfully refuse. Ultimately, in a case like this, it's *your* reputation and *your* honesty on the line. No job is worth compromising yourself to this degree. If you fear that your boss may fire you or punish you for not going along with him, document everything so that you can file a grievance and take this case to senior management or Human Resources.

If you see the boss say something that's not true or report something that is not accurate, then you have a more complicated choice. Do you stay out of the loop or blow the whistle? Again, it all depends on the ramifications of the dishonesty involved and your personal sense of what's important. One possible "middle course" might be to speak to the boss privately and let him know that you're uncomfortable with his dishonesty. You might also compare notes with your coworkers. Do they perceive the dishonesty? What do *they* think should be done or said? How does it affect *them*? Perhaps you could approach the boss as a delegation, asking him please not to misrepresent your department in the future.

When the Boss Is Not So Smart

Just because your boss holds the reins of power does not mean she's necessarily the sharpest tool in the shed. Many bosses lack good judgment, discernment, foresight, and simple brainpower. The question of how unintelligent people rise to become bosses in the first place is too big for us to cover here, but you know it happens.

When you're working for a boss who's not so smart, you and others often find that you have to compensate for

66 99   Advice for managers: Make time for introspection.

One of the primary keys to being an effective manager is introspection. It is essential that you understand yourself, your motivations, your strengths, and your weaknesses. You must constantly reinforce what you like about yourself and change what you do not.

Introspection requires you to see yourself clearly, not only as you see yourself in the mirror and in the echo chamber of your head, but also as your employees see you. It means being willing and able to admit and analyze your shortcomings, and adjust your behavior in response. It also means knowing what you do best and making the most of it.

This is important for anyone, but even more so for managers because the consequences of not understanding yourself at least as well as you understand balance sheets and market trends can be disastrous for everyone around you.

his deficiencies. Let's hope he'll be at least smart enough to realize how dependent he is on his underlings; otherwise you and your coworkers may have to be downright sneaky in getting things done the *right* way, rather than *his* way.

Don't blame your boss for not being smarter. Chances are he's doing the best he can. Don't expect insight or inspired leadership from such a boss. Don't expect such a boss to anticipate your needs. Be communicative and patient.

At best, a less-than-brilliant boss can still be honest and hardworking and fair-minded. Be grateful for those qualities. Genius isn't all it's cracked up to be anyway. (Refer to The Visionary in Chapter 4.) Just make sure you know the extent of your boss's limitations, and make adjustments for them.

When the Boss Is "in Crisis"

Your boss is human and has problems like everyone else. Occasionally the boss may face very big problems. Perhaps a close family member has just died or a child is in trouble.

When your boss is going through a personal crisis, you need to afford her the same patience and understanding that you would expect if the person in crisis were you. It's really that simple. If you know the boss is in crisis, try to refrain from making demands on her time and attention. Cut her a little slack if she seems forgetful. Be thoughtful and courteous.

A boss in crisis will certainly affect the entire office, but this need not precipitate a crisis if workers are mature enough not to take the boss's distracted or extrasensitive behavior personally. Be tolerant and empathic. This too shall pass.

When the Boss Gets Fired

The firing of your immediate boss can throw your department or office into chaos. No one knows what to expect next. Is your job still secure? Who is the new boss going to be? How long will it be before you get a new boss, and what should you be doing in the meantime?

You may not know why upper management has chosen to let your boss go. If you liked him, it can be a traumatic situation. You may even feel, out of loyalty, that you should also leave the company. But don't be impulsive with a decision like this! Wait until the dust settles, both at work and in your emotions. Chances are your boss is okay. He probably got a fine severance package. If you quit, you will probably not be awarded a similar deal. Your job is to take care of yourself and trust your former boss will land on his feet. Feel free to call your boss and express your regrets about the situation, but try not to ally yourself with your deposed boss.

Update your resume. If the powers-that-be were unhappy with your boss, they may also be looking with a jaundiced eye at your whole department. Also, a brand-new boss may want to bring her own people in to replace the old order. So, without being unduly paranoid, be ready for anything.

Just Do Your Work   Continue being productive. If you have work, do it. Don't slack off because there's no one to whom you're directly accountable now. Make sure that the mission of your office proceeds as usual, and that you don't give upper management any good reason to let you go.

Communicate with upper management. In a responsible company, when your boss is fired, someone from senior management should call a meeting with your department to explain what's going on. So keep those lines of communication open. Ask the senior manager when you could talk further and what types of changes can be expected in the future.

Document all your completed work and be prepared to itemize your job duties for the new boss. Be ready to demonstrate your value to the company. Don't assume that anyone else knows what you do or what you've accomplished. Now more than ever, you need to take stock of your achievements and be prepared to talk about them. There may be an important crossroads ahead, and your survival—and even possible advancement—may depend on your willingness and ability to advocate for yourself.

66 99 | Advice for managers: Make time for introspection.

Justin Menkes runs a think tank / consultancy called the Executive Intelligence Group and is the author of the popular and invaluable book *Executive Intelligence*. On my radio show, he talked about what "executive intelligence" means, beginning with the fundamental understanding that, as a boss, you are not the Lone Ranger.

"You can't possibly execute a strategy effectively if you don't understand how to do so through other people. It sounds so obvious and simple, but it's a rule violated day and night by ignorant and/or arrogant business managers.

We act naturally in ways that make us horrible executives. For example, the brain is hard-wired to jump to instant conclusions, which was essential for primitive humans to survive against the constant physical threats of the natural world. But in a complex business environment, that instant knee-jerk reaction can really get us into trouble. The most skilled executives take a moment or two to ask the right questions, probe a bit. Often on the surface a situation may appear to be one thing, but in actuality it's something else."

INTELLIGENCE CAN BE TAUGHT

Menkes makes the explosive point that even though executive intelligence can be taught, it doesn't usually develop naturally. Instead it has aspects that are counterintuitive, which is why it's so rare to find executives and administrators practicing it. That's also why those of us who master executive intelligence tend to rise above the pack. It turns out that executive intelligence goes against the grain of our human instincts. Using your team strategically and refraining from impulsive judgment are only two of the many facets of executive intelligence. Introspection is another.

In Summary: Like the rest of us, your boss has quirks, but is, more likely
Managing Up than not, a decent human being. The majority of bosses
are much more interested in getting the job done and
providing a positive environment for their workers than
in lording power over other people, making their workers unhappy, or conquering the world. Because they're
human, bosses come with a combination of qualities,
some good and some bad. So a word to the wise: Don't
decide that your boss is one type or another, and over-
look what may be positive aspects in her overall approach.
Try to keep an open mind and an inclusive perspective.

That said, there are certainly a lot of crummy, irresponsible bosses out there, and nothing makes an office
more dysfunctional than a bad boss. If your manager isn't
clear or consistent about expectations or misses meetings
so problems aren't addressed in a timely fashion, before
you know it you may be faced with an impossible deadline that could have been avoided. You have to work late
all week, compromising your relationships with your
family, your significant other, and your friends. You suffer
sleepless nights, headaches, depression, and possibly even
physical, stress-related illness.

Sadly, despite all the books and all the seminars and
workshops on better management, many managers don't
get the on-the-job training they need to do their job well.
It doesn't necessarily mean they're not well intentioned.
They're just unprepared for their responsibilities. And the
less able they are to manage you, the more you have to
manage them. Katherine Crowley, who introduced us to
the concept of "unhooking" in Chapter 3, calls this practice *managing up*.

Take Care of   The key to managing up is, first and foremost, to take
Yourself good care of yourself emotionally and physically. Second, even though you are not in charge, take the initiative when it comes to managing your relationship with
your boss. As Michael Feiner says in *The Feiner Points of*

Leadership, "Everyone has the ability to influence the quality and effectiveness of their relationship with their boss—no matter how insufferable he or she is." Although this may sound infeasible, just a few simple steps will put you on the road to managing your manager.

Most important, do your job so well that your manager has nothing to complain about. This should be your work ethic in any case, but *especially* with a bad manager, it gives you power and solid ground to stand on. Document your work so that your contribution and your value are undeniable.

Politely persist in asking for regular (at least weekly) status meetings to keep your boss on track and to reinforce the continuity of your day-to-day objectives and priorities. Use these meetings to clarify your expectations and get the boss to agree with them as though they were his or her idea, using language such as: "So, you want to review and sign off on those flow charts every Friday after lunch?" However you do it, it is vital to establish a dialogue with your boss—a dialogue with clear parameters and a clear focus on salient work-related topics. As an added benefit, this is the kind of behavior that will get you promoted into management. You don't have to have an actual leadership position to act like a leader.

If you have a boss who is impossible, you can find strength in numbers. You might get a number of people in your office together and collectively draw up a list or protocol for a healthier, more collaborative feedback-oriented relationship with your supervisor and senior management.

Symptoms of Bad Boss Behavior

- He demands you undertake impossible jobs.
- She's rude and insulting.
- He's moody and expects everyone in the office to mirror his moods.
- She plays favorites with your office mates.
- He ignores your needs and requests.

Treatments

- Find alternatives to unreasonable requests.
- Stand up for yourself, politely but firmly.
- Understand your emotions and the fact that they don't depend on anyone else's mood.
- Maintain strong, professional relations with your coworkers.
- Document your needs and requests and make them repeatedly, politely, and professionally.

6 gender politics in the workplace

Women at Work The growth of a large female work force over the past several generations has catalyzed fundamental changes in the nature of workplace relationships and power dynamics. Some hidden conflicts have become more readily apparent, while new forms of conflict have arisen, such as issues pertaining to gender balance in spheres of authority and competition between men for the attention of women at work or vice versa.

Of course, the ascent of women in professional circles has also had a humanizing influence. Behavior now understood as sexual harassment was once commonplace and accepted. No more. Also, the presence of women has done much to temper the testosterone-driven, often harsh atmosphere of the "man's world" of business. Though it is not politically correct to talk a lot about gender differences, some stereotypes about women and men do have a basis in reality. One such feature is that women are more relationship-oriented, while men tend to be preoccupied with ambition. Therefore, the influx of more women into the workplace may afford emotion a larger, more readily acknowledged place in day-to-day life on the job.

There are always exceptions to any generality, particularly gender-based ones. But there can be no denying that although women used to have to navigate through a man's world in business it is now a woman's world as well. This has brought a whole new set of emotional challenges.

However, while the field of play has changed for everyone concerned—both men and women—women still face the steepest challenges. Summing up the plight of women in the work force, former U.S. ambassador to Switzerland Faith Whittlesey once said, "Remember, Ginger Rogers did everything Fred Astaire did, but she did it backwards and in high heels."

A Little Background   In the early decades of capitalism in Europe and America, many of the workers in mills and factories were women, many of them in their teens and twenties. During World War II, married (and single) women worked the factories while men fought the war. Once the war was over, most women in the work force put their aprons back on so the men could have their jobs back. Women were then expected to fill the vast secretarial pools that characterized the era's new bureaucracies and corporations. Although these women were crucial to the success of their companies, they were paid poorly and treated as disposable—and often as sex objects—in most businesses.

Before the 1960s, the man of the house typically worked nine to five to support his family while the woman stayed home. As more women started working outside the home in new roles they wanted the option of a career. The Women's Liberation Movement was about serious issues: Women couldn't get "real" jobs in the marketplace because "all" they'd ever done was housework and raising kids. Housework wasn't considered real work and was not regarded as job experience. Women couldn't get credit in their own names because the family credit cards were always in their husband's name, leaving the wives with no independent credit history. This could be disastrous after a divorce. The ex-wives couldn't buy cars or sign leases on apartments.

Things have gotten much better. Today, despite continuing salary disparities, more women are in the workplace. But it hasn't been an easy ride.

In the early 1970s, California folksinger Bonnie Lockhart wrote a song called "Still Ain't Satisfied," which became a minor anthem of the national women's rights movement. The song begins:

> *Well, they've got women on TV*
> *And I still ain't satisfied*
> *'Cause cooptation's all I see*
> *And I still ain't satisfied*
> *They call me Ms.*
> *They sell me blue jeans*
> *They call it "Women's Lib"*
> *They make it sound obscene . . .*

Lockhart's song resonated with many thousands of women, who perceived that their newly minted "liberation" was riddled with contradictions and laden with shackles of a different kind. Women now had access to the birth control pill and legal abortion, but they were also pressured and expected by men to be much more sexually open than they had been in the past, whether they wanted to be or not. Women were now working many of the same jobs as men, but for less pay. To this day, a woman still only makes, on average, 77 cents for every dollar a man makes. (However, this stark discrepancy is a gross comparison of the median wages for all working men and women. In fact, according to the online CNN column "Everyday Money," when women work alongside men in the same shop, doing the same work, and employing the same skill sets, they are generally able to draw equitable salaries these days.)

Advertisers in particular were rabid in their often coarse and offensive attempts to exploit the new woman's independence to sell her everything from clothes to cars to candy. In the 1960s, Virginia Slims aired a series of TV commercials featuring a sultry, fashionably dressed woman, smiling airily and walking confidently toward the camera as she reaches inside her garment for her pack of cigarettes. Graciously and expertly she taps out a cigarette and raises it slowly to her sensual impeccably made-up mouth as the camera pans in on her perfect face. The jingle goes:

> *You've come a long way, baby,*
> *To get where you got to today.*
> *You've got your own cigarette now, baby,*
> *You've come a long, long way.*

Just in case anyone missed the point, the cooing female voiceover states that Virginia Slims cigarettes represent "the taste for today's woman."

These and other advertisements were emblematic of the hypersexual spin that the media placed on the women's rights movement that blossomed in the sixties and seventies.

But the reality was not so glamorous. Women had to work long hours for less-than-adequate pay. Ultimately, many women had to choose between family and career, and regardless of which choice they made, they were left with a nagging sense of loss and ambivalence.

The expectations placed on women, as well as the expectations women placed on themselves, became impossible. As writer Marya Mannes explained, "Nobody objects to a woman being a good writer or sculptor or geneticist if at the same time she manages to be a good wife, a good mother, good-looking, good-tempered, well-dressed, well-groomed, and unaggressive."

Sexual Politics The word *politics* has many meanings. One of my favorite definitions, from the *Random House Webster's College Dictionary* is "the use of strategy or intrigue in obtaining power, control, or status." In a sense, we're all engaged in "politics" all the time because power, control, and status

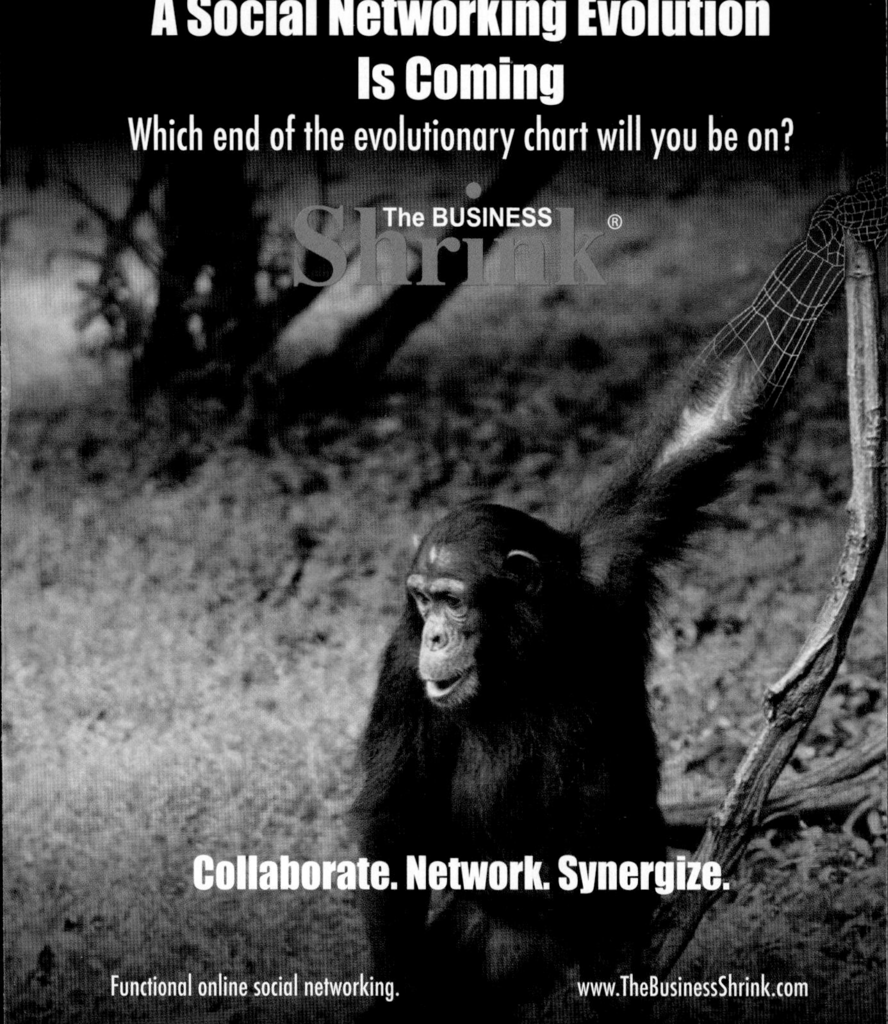
A Social Networking Evolution
Is Coming
Which end of the evolutionary chart will you be on?
The BUSINESS Shrink ®
Collaborate. Network. Synergize.
Functional online social networking.
www.TheBusinessShrink.com

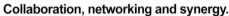

are things we all need to some degree, especially in our work life.

But introducing gender differences into the equation brings in an extra dimension, because the rules for gaining power, status, and control are different for women than they are for men. As author Lois Wyse has pointed out, "Men are taught to apologize for their weaknesses, women for their strengths." Also, women have access to different *types* of power and control than men.

We spoke earlier of stereotypes that have some basis in reality, and here's another one: Generally speaking, men are more interested in exercising power over others than women are. As a result, women, more often than not, have to be most careful in the arena of sexual politics.

Sexual Harassment   Sexual harassment laws were not on the books in the sixties or early seventies. Though the Civil Rights Act of 1964 prohibited "discrimination at work on the basis of race, color, religion, national origin and sex," sexual harassment per se was never legally recognized as discrimination until a 1976 lower court ruling in Washington, D.C. (*Williams v. Saxbe*). In the years that followed, several courts issued rulings that categorized sexual harassment as prohibited discrimination, Illinois banned sexual harassment of state employees, and Congress convened hearings on the subject of sexual harassment. Then in the 1986 ruling in the case of *Meritor Savings v. Vinson*, the U.S. Supreme Court declared, "A claim of hostile environment sexual harassment is a form of sex discrimination that is actionable under Title VII [of the 1964 Civil Rights Act]; the language of Title VII is not limited to 'economic' or 'tangible' discrimination . . ."

It had taken decades, but the reality of sexual harassment as a legitimate and serious grievance, meriting legal remedies, was at last firmly established.

There were, however, legions of untold workplace casualties along the way, as there have continued to be in

Going for Partnership

Imagine Gloria calls me from her downtown office in Cleveland and says, "Peter, I've been with this law firm for nine years, and I've worked my butt off. My record is outstanding; we've prevailed in every case that I've worked on that's ever gone to trial. Now they have two openings at the equity partnership tier in my firm. I'm competing with five guys for those two spaces."

ME: Well, technically that gives you one chance in three, all other things being equal.

GLORIA: But all things are *not* equal! I've been here the longest of all those guys. And no one has a record of success that's as consistent as mine!

ME: Well, then, what are you worried about? Sounds to me like you're a slam dunk for that partnership position.

GLORIA: Yeah, but the problem is, they've never *had* a female partner before in this firm. And the scuttlebutt I'm picking up from the grapevine is that they don't mean to start now. The old guys who run this firm are stuffy old school and set in their ways. They're afraid that having my name listed as a partner might "soften' their image somehow.

ME: Well, listen, you're an advocate, right? Now's your chance to advocate for *yourself.*

GLORIA: How do you suggest I do that? This office has a veneer of informality, but in actuality there are more protocols here than the United Nations. I don't *dare* go to one of the partners and make a case for myself. That'll disqualify me right away.

ME: Well, then, what are your options, Gloria? Are you just going to wait and see what happens? From what you're telling me, it's all over if you do that.

GLORIA: Yeah, I'm afraid that's true.

ME: Who decides who gets promoted to partner at your firm? All the partners do, right? There must be *one* partner there you can talk to—or at least one partner you know appreciates your work. You don't have to canvass all your bosses. Just go in there and talk to someone and make sure you're not overlooked here. This is not the time to pretend that you're invisible, Gloria. What can they do—fire you? After all this time, I doubt that very much. It would not be in their best interests.

GLORIA: Well . . . I wouldn't want them to feel like I was threatening them.

ME: *What?* Gloria, I'm not saying you should bring a gun when you talk to the guy.

GLORIA: Yeah, but with my seniority, and my track record, I have a *right* to be promoted to partner. And what could threaten them is, if they don't make me a partner, I *could* sue for unfair discrimination on the basis of gender, a violation of my civil rights.

louts; they are sophisticated, well-dressed, well-spoken professional men, but their conversation quickly devolves into snickering. When our main character happens to walk by and ask them a question, she excuses herself for interrupting their conversation, and one of them replies that she shouldn't worry, they hadn't been discussing anything important, just making idle talk about the details of one of Michael's (her boyfriend's) cases. "Drilling rights," adds the other man, by way of explanation.

Sexual Power   The flip side of sexual harassment is sexual power. This means using one's ability to appear attractive and excite sexual interest as a means of gaining favorable notice and, ultimately, some measure of control or authority. Women tend to wield this power more than men do—not because women are inherently manipulative creatures, and certainly not because women have more sexual feelings than men do, but because women in business use what resources they have at their command, just as men do. A woman may fail to get a boss's attention or influence team decision-making by being smart. If, however, she presents her ideas wrapped in a subtle fragrance of flirtation, she may be more likely to have her suggestions adopted by the team and may even be considered a stronger candidate for promotion at a later date.

It's a dangerous game, and many (probably most) women are allergic to it. If they try to do it unskillfully, without a great deal of confidence and poise, it can backfire and have negative social, emotional, and professional consequences. It is also a balancing act; women have to be careful not to send the wrong message and must turn off the charm in a heartbeat if an undesirable suitor starts to feel seriously encouraged. Many women have an instinct for this art, but others overplay their hand, and men notice.

A friend told me about an exchange he once had in an office where only one woman was on staff. The woman was the most popular person at the job—bright and attractive—though at first no one paid a great deal of attention to her substantial professional skills. Soon she saw that with just a little flattery and a measured dose of flirtation every day, she could butter up her coworkers. But some of the men began to sense a certain calculated quality to her unflappably sunny demeanor. A colleague took my friend aside one day and commented wryly, "I bet Jackie comes in wearing a dress tomorrow to capitalize on her capital games of today." This man was resentful. He'd asked Jackie out and been turned down. Now he was cynical about her style of collegial pleasantness.

Of course, men also use their sexual power to gain attention and influence. But the point is, *men don't have to do it*, because they have other natural sources of credibility and clout at their command, such as louder, deeper voices and a firmly embedded cultural bias and deference toward them. You don't believe it? Then why, as of this writing, has there not yet been a woman president?

So if you're a male who thinks your office mate is an unconscionable flirt (or worse yet, a "tease"), cut her some slack and have some sympathy. She may be playing games, but she sure didn't write the rulebook.

When Women Compete with One Another

Men and women are raised to handle conflict and competition differently. Men learn to expect competition in all facets of life and consequently tend to be more comfortable with it in their personal relationships. Men tend to be direct with each other when there's a conflict.

Women, on the other hand, get messages early on and throughout life that the only good relationships with other women are free of conflict, supportive, and generally positive at all times. So when they compete or conflict with each other at work, they are less sure how to deal with it because they never had early training, that early and easy familiarity with competition and conflict.

Going Behind Each Other's Backs

Many women end up competing behind each other's backs in a way that appears as though they're not really competing at all. Those women are stuck in an antiquated idea of how nice girls must act: never in-your-face. However, there are high-profile women who have had the moxie to begin to change that nice façade. Confrontation is now okay for women at work. As women evolve in the workplace, there are numerous examples of high-powered women who exercise what used to be considered male gender-specific traits and are now widely recognized as gender-neutral. These women are able to be overtly tough and still maintain their femininity. But it's not easy. A lot of people still characterize such pioneering women as "masculine."

Still in the majority of cases, conflict between two women is likely to be more subtle and surreptitious than conflict between two men or between a man and woman. That makes it harder to see there is a problem, and consequently, more difficult to handle, because you're not quite sure what's going on. Let's call it the "Did she really say that about me?" factor.

Answering this question on my radio show was Nan Mooney, author of *I Can't Believe She Did That! Why Women Betray Other Women at Work.* "Most girls these days grow up doing sports, but one of the dangers is that we don't know how to deal with conflict in our personal relationships. Of course the relationships we have with our work colleagues are personal. They're not the same as private friendships, but they're certainly not the same as being on a sports field either. They're somewhere in the middle. I think that is important, but I don't think it's something that has to start happening at age six or it's all over. I think that women in the workplace now just need to be more aware when these dynamics come up and to communicate with one another when there's a problem, even though it can feel dangerous and like the other woman might get angry or feel hurt."

"Is It Harassment If She Doesn't Mind?"

Laura goes to her boss, Lena, and says she has a complaint about sexual harassment in the office.

"It's Dennis," explains Laura. "I have to work around him and Cynthia every day, and he's always making sexually loaded comments that are disturbing to her and to me as well."

"How do you know he's bothering Cynthia?" asks Lena. "Does she say so?"

"You know, Cynthia keeps her thoughts to herself. She doesn't want to rock the boat. But the whole thing just sets up an upsetting dynamic for everyone around. Cynthia walks in, Dennis says 'Hi, Cutie,' in this insinuating tone and looks her up and down. And I'm sitting right there too. It's uncomfortable."

Lena asks, "Are you sure Cynthia's not egging him on in any way? I mean, if *she's* not complaining . . . ?"

"I'm positive!" declares Laura. "Cynthia minds her own business. She just looks away. You can ask her."

"Well, I should do that," agrees Lena.

Lena summons Cynthia into her office for a private conference. She tells Cynthia, "I've heard from some people in the office that Dennis makes suggestive, unwelcome comments to you on a daily basis. Is that true?"

Cynthia glances down. She appears unsure of herself.

Lena hesitates. Cynthia is a shy, unassertive young woman. This must be difficult for her.

Finally Cynthia says, "Well, he flirts with me a little. But I don't mind."

"You don't?"

Cynthia shakes her head.

"Honestly, Cynthia. It's okay with you that Dennis flirts with you every day?" Lena is certain Cynthia cannot be attracted to Dennis, an overweight fifty-five-year-old.

Cynthia shrugs. "It doesn't bother me. I've heard worse. I like Dennis. He's nice. He doesn't mean any harm."

"I see." Lena folds her arms. "You don't flirt back with him though, do you?"

Cynthia blushes. "No," she says. "Definitely not. I don't like him—that way."

"Well." Lena leans forward. "If you want, I can say something to him and ask him to stop flirting with you. Even if you don't mind it that much, it's not really appropriate for him to make suggestive comments just because you're an attractive young woman."

"I don't want to get him in trouble," says Cynthia quickly. "And if you say something to him, he'll be mad at me. And actually . . ." Cynthia bites her lip, hesitating to say what she has to say next. But she plunges ahead. "Actually, I think it's more of a problem for Rochelle and Laura, because they're always right there in the room. I can tell it bothers *them* when they hear it. But it doesn't bother me. I think it's kind of sweet. Really—he doesn't threaten me or anything. He's not obscene. He just compliments me on my appearance really."

Lena sighs. "I still think it's obnoxious behavior, Cynthia, frankly. And since he is bugging Laura and Rochelle, I am going to talk to him anyway and ask him to tone it down. We can't have a situation where some people in the office are being made to feel uncomfortable by his behavior. Don't worry; I'll make sure he understands it isn't your fault." ■

It's not so much that certain career paths or companies or jobs for women require them to become more direct or forward or ready for battle. In fact, differences between women seem to arise much more frequently in environments that are still mostly male and where most of the power is still in the hands of men. In those environments, Mooney believes, an unstated, unacknowledged feeling often exists that there isn't room for many women, and so a "her-or-me" situation is established. Then women tend not to be generous and communicative with the other women working around them. A woman may even try to sabotage another woman employee or make her look bad because she's afraid that if the other woman looks too good or if she helps her out, she may wind up getting the axe.

Indirect Competition: A Case in Point   Mooney shared a story from her own life that illustrates this type of dynamic. In fact, this was the very incident that got her interested in the subject of woman-to-woman interactions at work.

"It happened at a job I had shortly out of college. I was working in the sound business in Los Angeles with a colleague. I was an assistant, and I had a female colleague who was an assistant to somebody else in the same office. It was a very top-heavy organization, and we both were beginning to figure out that there wasn't much room for us to move up. We started talking a little back and forth about moving on and that kind of thing. I decided to make the move to leave, and I was looking for new jobs and talking to people and checking things out. She started asking me about it, and so I started sharing information, and she was very supportive, saying things like, 'That sounds great, you should apply for this,'—that sort of thing.

"Finally, after a lot of searching around, I found a job that I thought would be really good for me and sent in my application. It was in New York, so I flew there to interview and then came back. And then I got a phone call from them: it was down to three people.

"Then one day I walked into the office and my colleague sort of cleared her throat and said, 'I need to tell you something.' I said okay, and she said, 'I applied for that job too, and I'm one of those three people it's down to.'

"I was so flabbergasted. Not by the fact that she had applied for the job but that she had been so secretive about it and had never let on, until it was basically impossible for her to hide it any longer, and the fact that she had been pumping me for information. I felt so betrayed by her lack of communication. In that situation I really felt like she'd taken advantage of me. And at that young age I had no idea how to deal with it, what to say to her or anything."

Today, Mooney would be much more direct about letting her colleague know that her behavior was disrespectful and unfair. But at the time, like many women, Mooney felt like she had done something wrong, as if she had been stupid to share the information in the first place.

A Poisoned Atmosphere   Was she angry? Vindictive? Did she seek revenge? Angry, yes, and stunned. She had been utterly unprepared for the possibility that another woman would do something like that. As she says, "I think I would not have been so shocked if that had happened with a man, because I was more prepared in my mind for the fact that men are competitive in the workplace."

In the end, the third woman got the job, but you can imagine the atmosphere in the office after that. Mooney and her colleague had to continue working together with this betrayal lying between them. Neither of them knew what to say about it or how to address it. So they never said another word about it, but the closeness and camaraderie they had once shared was completely destroyed.

Mooney's story is one example of the many ways in which women compete. Mooney might have felt entirely differently toward her colleague had she been more forthright early on and told her that she, too, was interested in the job. Then, conceivably, Mooney might have taken an attitude of "may the best woman win."

For women, job-site competitiveness can be indirect to the point of cattiness and outright backstabbing. It's not that men don't do these things, but they also naturally bond and become buddies in a way that's more accepting of adversarial situations. They can separate and compartmentalize these different levels of relationship. Among both women and men, however, a lot of defensive, indirect, even underhanded behavior stems from insecurity.

But still in many situations where a lot of women are working together, everyone feels a great deal of pressure to be super-nice and super-supportive. They may hesitate to raise an issue for fear of looking like the bad person. Even simple disagreement or dissent may be seen as "too aggressive" or hostile.

At least right now, many women in the workplace tend to err on the side of caution when the inevitable competition or conflict arises. But like everything else, this is rapidly changing. Women tend to be fast learners (yes, faster than men, because they have to be). My bet is that gender-specific modes of workplace conflict will soon be a relic of the past.

Women in Charge

Though they are becoming ever more common, woman bosses face unique challenges. They often have to be extra-tough in order to be taken seriously. Even women in high-level executive positions are sometimes mistaken for administrative assistants by visiting CEOs or business leaders. Men are still most comfortable with other men in the boardroom and executive suites. Therefore, businesswomen in positions of power generally have to assert themselves more forcefully than men do.

And men have to get used to it.

My friend Robert was the producer of a news show at a radio station in New York City. He had just hired a new reporter to support the show. The reporter was one of those living, breathing Big Apple stereotypes, constantly on the lookout for a Big Story, and a hot woman.

Robert, whose dry Southern wit included a mischievous nature, walked the reporter into the newsroom and over to a square glass booth that provided a quiet work zone. When Robert and his brash new hire got to the glass booth, Robert opened the door. There before them sat a striking woman, who had been seated and looking in the opposite direction. She abruptly turned, rose from her chair to her full six feet, and looked the new guy in the eye as Robert made the usual introductions. The reporter was discombobulated to suddenly find himself up close to a stunning blonde—and even more stunned to learn that she was his new boss!

The new reporter hadn't had a woman boss since he'd left his mother's house at age nineteen. He experienced a rush of conflicting feelings: lust, embarrassment, and perhaps a touch of fear.

A short while later, Robert took the reporter aside, smiled paternally, and said drolly, "Yup, that's Annabelle. She's gorgeous and brilliant. Get over the 'gorgeous' part. Keep your eyes on hers when she talks to you, and pay attention. She doesn't have time to train men how to take orders from women."

Unfortunately, not every man who works for a female boss has a wise mentor like Robert around to spell out the situation.

The Glass Ceiling   Female bosses are still much scarcer than male bosses. In the highest echelons of corporate hierarchy, women are very rare indeed. According to Catalyst, an organization devoted to studying women in the workplace, only about

16 percent of corporate officers at *Fortune* 500 companies are female. And according to Carol Bartz, CEO of the international software company Autodesk, only 2 percent of *Fortune* 500 CEOs are women.

Similarly, Catalyst reports that of the *Fortune* 500 companies, only 14.7 percent have a board of directors that is chaired by a woman. Fifty-three *Fortune* 500 companies have no women board members at all, while 182 *Fortune* 500 companies have only one female director. Given that corporate boards play a critical role in recruiting CEOs and other top executives, it is easy to see that a very real "old boys' club" still exists in America's highest levels of corporate culture.

Still, there are a number of high-profile female CEOs in the United States, such as Patricia A. Woertz of Archer Daniels Midland, Indra Nooyi of PepsiCo, and Irene B. Rosenfeld of Kraft Foods. While still a minority, their numbers are growing, and their influence is slowly but surely changing the world of big business.

Women Managers and the Impostor Syndrome

One negative thinking pattern in particular has attracted much attention from workplace psychologists and is a topic I've addressed several times on my radio show. That is the Impostor Syndrome. In shrink lingo, people with Impostor Syndrome are unable to internalize their accomplishments. In human-speak, they feel like fakes.

Research has shown that the Impostor Syndrome seems to affect women more than men. One of those researchers, Caitlin Friedman, author of *The Girl's Guide to Being a Boss (Without Being a Bitch)*, told my listeners that one of the reasons for this is that women in management and in executive suites are still a relatively new phenomenon. Because of this novelty, women have not had the advantage of learning from the other female bosses who have gone before them.

Caitlin Friedman told my listeners:

A lot of women, especially in leadership positions, suffer from Impostor Syndrome. They feel like they are unworthy and that their success is just because of good luck and not hard work. I used to have a lot of feelings like that, especially when I was delegating to someone. I'd have feelings like, "Who am I to delegate, and why is she going to listen to me?"

In my case and among the women I've interviewed, a lot of [female supervisors] feel like there was an emotional expectation that their employees had of them, an expectation that men just don't face. They expected their women bosses to be more understanding and more conscious of work/life balance issues, and more engaged on a friendship level, which makes it very difficult when you're a manager.

Women need to define their own success. They should have a hundred percent choice in how they define themselves as successful people. If that's staying at home with their kids, then that's an amazing job. If it's going back to the office, if it's starting a business out of their home, I think those are great things too. We need to support and encourage women to make choices that are right for themselves, and not judge them.

FACT AND FICTION **FICTION:** The results of the Women's Liberation Movement of the 1960s and 1970s were all great for women.
FACT: The Women's Liberation Movement turned out to be a mixed blessing for women. Women were admitted in greater numbers into the work force but often expected to do the same work as men for less pay. Birth control became widely available, but then women also faced increased pressure to be sexually available to men.

FICTION: Now that sexual harassment laws are on the books, women are protected and don't have to worry about sexual harassment at work.
FACT: Sexual harassment in the workplace is still an epidemic problem, despite the law.

FICTION: Women are sweet and naturally never compete with each other.

FACT: Women may be conditioned to feel that they should not compete, but women do compete with each other, sometimes in indirect ways (if they feel they have to hide their ambition).

FICTION: Women who try to use their ability to appear attractive as a means of gaining power at work are unethical and diabolically manipulative.

FACT: Everyone has to use the resources at hand. Sometimes women face a terrible dilemma; they cannot gain leverage or attention with their ideas at work unless they "play the game" of dressing attractively and flattering men.

FICTION: Now that so many women hold professional positions in America, women have just as much access to power and privilege as men do.

FACT: It's still largely a "man's world" in terms of work, and woman are regularly passed over for promotions that should rightfully be theirs but are instead awarded to men. Corporate America is still largely controlled by men. The corporate boards of America are dominated by men.

Characteristics of Powerful Women

Newsweek published an intriguing article in which the magazine profiled twenty businesswomen, asking them what it's like to be in charge. They picked women in the arts as well as business. What seemed to bind many of these women together was the way they faced their fears of rising and excelling, not just in a man's world but in any environment. They sometimes felt afraid, but they nonetheless did what they had to do. They had a can-do attitude. They were self-reliant. They kept raising their own bars for achievement before anyone needed to do it for them. They seized new opportunities boldly, and even when those opportunities didn't pan out, somehow they found themselves farther ahead. When they stumbled and fell, they picked themselves up and kept charging forward.

This type of spirited attitude was much rarer in women, many of whom had never experienced school team sports. This is where most boys learn not only about the mystical union of teammates but also how to get up when they're knocked down and continue to improve. The locker room lesson is to come back and come back and come back, over and over.

Fortunately, the post–women's liberation generation has had the opportunity to enjoy the same team sports that boys do, thanks to a famous 1972 amendment to the Civil Rights Act, known as Title IX. Title IX stipulates that public schools cannot exclude girls from any of the sporting activities they provide for boys. Indirectly, Title IX has actually been a huge help to women in management.

Still, by and large, women are generally more interested in discussing feelings than football. Men find it easier to express anger than women do. As noted at the beginning of this chapter, men tend to think more about their goals and ambitions, while women are more relationship-oriented. Men need to get more in touch with their feelings, and women need to assert themselves with more confidence. These generalizations are not always true, but they often are.

In business, women face special challenges because of the ways they are socialized, but in life, men are hobbled by the expectation that they shouldn't be as emotional as women. In fact, all of us are emotional, though we can't always show it. Many men today were brought up with the mantra, "Boys don't cry." Thankfully, this type of "male conditioning" has begun to fall out of favor; still women have a lot to teach men about the life of the heart. If they can bring those lessons more fully into the workplace, everyone will benefit, and no doubt so will the bottom line.

Symptoms of Gender Problems in the Workplace

- There are obvious differences in the pay and working conditions for men and women.
- Sexual innuendo is widespread and tolerated by management.
- Women employees are defensive and engage in backstabbing each other while competing for positions or projects.
- Some women openly flirt with male employees to get what they want.

Treatments

- Document any discrimination in the workplace and bring it to the attention of management. Consult an attorney for an educated legal opinion.
- Stand up to sexual harassment and bring it to the attention of management with a request that the company intervene to end the harassment. Sexual harassment isn't just unpleasant; it's illegal.
- As a female employee, be open and honest in your relationships with other female workers, just as with all employees.
- If you flirt to get what you want, be careful. Tactics like that can backfire. It's much better to engage your colleagues on a professional level.

7 healthy relationships in the workplace

Creating a Positive Work Environment

Enlightened companies realize that the key to avoiding negativity and disgruntled employees is to always work toward a more positive work environment. This is not only the responsibility of management, however—it's up to each of us. Most negativity can be avoided if we are consistently conscious and proactive about being positive. Then the inevitable periodic conflict that humans create becomes much easier to see coming and to manage, because respect and trust have already been established.

Encourage

Maybe you've heard the old office chant, "Don't give me praises; give me raises." It's only half true. People need praise, too. Don't you feel like a million dollars when someone sincerely compliments your work? Wouldn't you like to give that feeling to others?

Here is a simple principle: Encourage, don't disparage. When people are recognized for their good ideas, a self-perpetuating cycle begins and more good ideas are generated. If you are solidly grounded in your own personal and professional sense of security and are emotionally healthy, you won't feel threatened by anyone else's success. Few things spoil a work environment more than belittling or minimizing other people's contributions.

Encourage, as you would like to be encouraged. Giving genuine praise may feel awkward at first, but it will quickly become a habit, and an authentic expression of who you are. People will be more drawn to you than ever, and you will become an early choice for any team or group activity.

Listen   Hands down, listening is the most important communication skill you can bring to your relationships and to your work environment. Good listening is the most underrated ability in the world, period. As Daniel Goleman succinctly states in *Working with Emotional Intelligence*, "Listening is essential for workplace success."

People absolutely need to be heard. Stop and think about it. Aren't the most popular people you know also some of the best listeners? This is no coincidence. Millions of people have the mistaken idea that the best way to gain favor is through extensive talking. Of course, it's nice to have entertaining things to say but, as a rule, it's

66 99 | Advice for managers: Let employees have a say.

Although money is important, it's often not the most important thing to employees. Certainly a raise or the prospect of a bonus is a great motivator, and people expect to earn a reasonable salary. But what really motivate people to do well are the less tangible rewards, such as collaboration, cooperation, pride in their work product, and teamwork. Also of enormous value is the chance for employees of all levels to have a say in decision-making. In this global economy with so many new ways of doing business, perhaps the single biggest motivator for most people is feeling that they are learning, growing, and developing skills every day—skills that will result in a job that is even more challenging and stimulating and, yes, that pays better.

Communication, community, and a sense of "being plugged in" are essential. As a manager, it is important to honor requests for one-on-one meetings and to provide team and/or individual reviews once a month, as well as continual feedback on projects. Set up situations where colleagues can get together and brainstorm. If there are opportunities to share ideas, people feel as if they're an integral part of a team. You can win the hearts and minds of your staff with genuine, open, honest communication and feedback.

much more important to show interest in what *other people* have to say.

Active listening is a skill that can be developed, though it requires a significant degree of observation and attention. We generally talk and listen at a rate of about 90 words a minute, but when we talk to ourselves in our minds, the rate is about 900 words a minute. So the relatively slow pace of human speech creates a sense of idle time in our minds that invites distraction. That's why good listening does not come as naturally as, say, breathing or talking.

But, like most skills, listening gets much easier once it becomes habitual. It takes concentration to develop your listening skills, but it's not difficult. Once you begin to get the hang of it, you will probably even find that it's fun. You'll notice things that would have passed you by before you started applying yourself to the art of listening.

THE DOS AND DON'TS OF LISTENING

- **DO** pay attention not only to the speaker's words, but also to his body language, tone, and facial expressions. Researchers estimate that roughly 70 percent of all communication is nonverbal. Tone and emotional cues are every bit as important, if not more so, than words.
- **DO NOT** zone out or get distracted by your own thoughts, though they may seem much more compelling than what the other person is saying. Daydreaming is a sin when your dialogue partner perceives it—and believe me, it shows. Your eyes rove or they glaze over, your fingers start dancing, or your verbal responses are inappropriate. Worst of all, you get stuck in an embarrassing pause and are forced to say, "I'm sorry. I missed that. Would you please repeat it?"
- **DO** occasionally paraphrase what the other person has said ("So you mean that . . ."). Especially in complex or emotionally charged conversation,

it gives the speaker a sense of reassurance to be clearly and accurately "reflected."

- **DO NOT** try to read the other person's mind or finish her thoughts for her. Don't make assumptions about where a person's sentence is going, what she will say next, or what she's "really" trying to say. Few things are more annoying than when somebody assumes they already know what you have to say before you've finished speaking. As you listen, remember that your preconceptions are far less important and generally much less correct than you might imagine.

- **DO** ask periodic questions that show you're interested, and demonstrate your desire to understand what the other person is telling you. Try to get a complete picture. Be curious. Don't riddle the other person with questions, but ask her periodically, perhaps during pauses in the conversation.

- **DO NOT** interrupt the other person midspeech, and do not give way to "easy" interruptions. Ignore your cell phone and your BlackBerry. If you have ever been telling someone something important, especially something difficult to say, only to have the other person's attention snatched away by ringing and beeping, then you know just how devastating such channel changing can be to your pride. Every time you take a call instead of continuing to actively listen to another person, it is the equivalent of getting up and walking out of the room midconversation.

- **DO** put yourself in the speaker's shoes. Consider what he is feeling. Think about his situation, where he is coming from, why he is having this conversation with you, and what he needs.

- **DO NOT** be quick to give advice or tell the other person how he should feel. Unsolicited advice is almost always unwelcome. People don't really want to be told what to do—they just want to be listened to and feel understood. That's the service you're providing when someone confides in you. But if you feel very strongly that you have important advice to give, at least ask permission. "Do you mind if I offer some advice about this?" And as for telling people what to feel, *never* do that under any circumstances! People will feel how they feel, and if you tell them they should feel differently you'll only succeed in making them feel worse.

- **DO** keep practicing and developing your active listening skills. It's a lifelong pursuit.

66 99 | **Advice for managers**: Recognize achievement.

Remarkably simple nonmonetary incentives can help keep employees happy. Awarding a special mention to a peak performer at a staff meeting or in a company newsletter may mitigate the inevitable frustrations and stresses of work and motivate workers to stay with their employer.

Have you ever seen an "Employee of the Month" plaque or picture in the lobby of a hotel? It may not have made an overwhelming impression on you, and in fact you may have even passed by the Employee of the Month in the hall the next morning and failed to recognize him or her. But you can bet that for the men and women who work at that hotel, this kind of public tribute is significant.

We all want to be recognized for our efforts. We want to feel as if our hard work is appreciated, and most of us want that appreciation to be very public. If a worker doesn't feel appreciated, he is much more likely to burn out.

Create ways of showing public appreciation for your outstanding workers. Make it something fun that everyone can share in, like the whole team celebrating the employee's good work over lunch at a restaurant of his choice. To avoid creating an overly competitive environment, make sure *everyone* who deserves it gets a little perk and some public praise now and again. It's a very cost-effective way to bolster morale.

Generate Trust   Trusting relationships are the heartbeat of a smooth-running, emotionally healthy workplace. Though some people inspire trust immediately (and others inspire just the opposite), trust usually takes a while to develop. Trust is fragile and earned by degrees. Just ask anyone who has cheated on his or her spouse and asked for forgiveness. Forgiveness? Maybe. Trust? Not a chance—maybe in fifteen years. The same holds true for someone who breaks trust in the office. Spilling company secrets to the

---

66 99   Advice for managers: Be open to multiple perspectives.

Some leaders surround themselves with people who only tell them what they want to hear. As Peter Senge cautions in *The Fifth Discipline*, "Nothing undermines openness more surely than certainty. Once we feel as if we have 'the answer,' all motivation to question our thinking disappears." The yes-ers shield their leaders from divergent points of view, which are essential for both personal growth and better decision-making.

The smartest leaders view situations from multiple perspectives. They solicit advice from a range of people whose intelligence they respect but whose temperament, knowledge, backgrounds, and approaches to life and work differ from their own. One person may be cautious and pragmatic, another daring and imaginative; one may have confidence in individual team members, another may be more aware of team members' shortcomings. Each perspective provides a piece of the whole picture.

Smart managers go deeper still, and analyze their advisors' agendas. Are they saying what they really think? We've all met individuals who are great at directly saying what they mean and others who are more circumspect. This does not mean that you should be paranoid and distrustful of your advisors; only that it is prudent to take into account their personalities and (possibly unconscious) motives at any given time.

But don't get so caught up in your psychological perceptions that you lose your warmth and respect for people. You don't want to be a Machiavellian Strategist!

competition is the equivalent of cheating on a spouse. Fail to make a crucial deadline after assuring your boss, "Don't worry. I've got you covered," and you will quickly see that regaining the boss's trust will be your second (unpaid) full-time job.

So once you've established trust, hold onto it dearly. Whatever you do, don't squander it because it is precious.

Trust begins with willingness—the willingness to trust and to be trustworthy. Trust at work is also predicated on the perception that other people are competent and can be depended on to perform their duties and follow through on their commitments. Additionally, trust includes a sense that other people are acting for the greater good.

Be Honest   In a trusting environment, people assume that their peers are honest. Honesty takes a number of forms.

INTELLECTUAL HONESTY   For an office to function optimally, colleagues must give each other credit where credit is due and never try to steal one another's ideas. If someone steals your ideas, or you steal theirs, trust is irreparably broken.

What can you do if someone steals your idea? First, take the appropriate steps to ensure that this never happens again. Do what you have to do to protect your information in the future. In fact, that is the first symptom of a breakdown in trust: the need for armor and protection, the expenditure of energy *against* the possibility of being mistreated or violated in some way. Next, you might inform your boss about the offender's infringement on your intellectual property. However, even though you can take these steps to protect yourself, there is no longer a solid foundation of emotional and professional safety in the work environment.

PERSONAL HONESTY   This means much more than simply telling the truth. It also means refraining from mean-spirited gossip around the water cooler and the lunch table. If you talk about a coworker behind her back in ways that you wouldn't to her face, you are engaging in a type of personal dishonesty that will sooner or later—usually sooner—destroy trust between you and that other person as well as have rippling detrimental effects on the entire workplace culture. So, to maintain an atmosphere of trust, avoid derogatory gossip, and do not tolerate it when you hear it from others. Politely but firmly nip it in the bud.

It's one thing to talk about each other in a spirit of excitement and interest. "Hey, did you see Mike's new car?" "Did you meet Frieda's new boyfriend?" That's not mean gossip. That's just a way of affirming that you care about each other, and you are a community. We all instinctively know the difference between talking about another person and gossiping about them in a belittling way. If you're not sure, check in with your gut.

SELF-HONESTY   Inevitably, there will be events, people, and circumstances that annoy you from time to time. Don't repress or deny these feelings. Don't try to sugarcoat your dissatisfaction or cover it up with a nice-nice attitude. Sometimes an atmosphere of rigid, unwavering sweetness can be as oppressive as raging conflict. So let your feelings show, at least to yourself. Be true to what's real for you.

At the same time, don't let those feelings get out of control or inflict themselves on unwilling coworkers. Instead, find a positive solution.

Let's say your supervisor has just suggested that everyone in your small office eat lunch together on Mondays, Wednesdays, and Fridays to strengthen your sense of team spirit and become better acquainted. Maybe this doesn't work for you. Maybe your quiet lunches are a big part of what sustains you through the day. So don't just go with the flow because it's what other people seem to expect. Don't tell yourself it's what you should do for the sake of the team. Listen to your feelings! Stick up for yourself, your needs, and your perceptions. Respectfully communicate to your team and your supervisor that it's important for you to have some alone time in the middle of the day. If possible, suggest some alternate activity that can help the team bond.

It's hard to trust others when you can't quite trust yourself. Self-honesty is a prerequisite to self-trust. If you're forthcoming about your feelings, that will make it easier for others to trust you as well.

66 99   **Advice for managers:** Lead in times of duress.

How does a good leader lead during times of institutional change mandated in the corporate food chain?

The same man who taught me about how to see value and wisdom in difficult people also taught me how to cope with such situations. When computers first arrived at his company, many employees were intimidated. My mentor attended the first set of classes with the other students—his employees. During the class breaks, he even took part in the grousing and complaining that always goes hand-in-hand with this type of unwelcome challenge. Everyone understood that the boss sympathized with their fears, and that he was taking note of their efforts to adapt.

When budget cuts were mandated, he would sit for hours explaining the pressures he was under and ask employees for their ideas about cutting costs. When he was forced to make the cuts, they understood that he had done his best to protect them. He was left with a staff saddened by the loss of friends but not resentful of his leadership or engaged in the kind of bitter emotional payback that often precedes layoffs.

My mentor demonstrated that, in the hardest of times, a good leader is not only frank with his workers, but he also gets right in the trenches with them and takes as much of the burden on as he feasibly can. It is during the tough times that a good leader is closest to his team and demonstrates through action that he cares about his team members' fate.

Personal Relationships in a Professional Environment

Some work relationships are neutral while others are loaded with emotional freight. More likely than not, no matter how professional you may be, over time you will develop relationships with coworkers that extend beyond the workplace. No matter how diligent you are about drawing a line between your personal and professional lives, these dynamics can complicate the business of getting things done.

Friends at Work

On the surface it may seem that friendships in the workplace are a good thing. They are certainly not an abnormal thing; friendships naturally form in an office environment. You work closely with someone for a while and, next thing you know, the seeds of a lifelong friendship have been planted.

While friendships at work can be positive, they need to be managed carefully during working hours. Coworkers who spend more time chatting about their weekends and *American Idol* than actually working often need to be separated like schoolchildren. Though it may seem churlish to complain about people getting along well, workplace friendships can negatively affect the bottom line.

No matter how discreet you may believe yourself to be, conflict has a trickle-down effect, and everybody's work is disrupted when tensions arise in the workplace. Conversely, it can be just as disruptive and distracting to work in close proximity to a clique of close friends engaged in personal discussions.

Understandably, people tend to value their friendships more than they do their work. This isn't necessarily bad, but it can lead to some questionable choices. If you come to work one day and a project as well as a friend needs your immediate attention, which do you choose? Whatever choice you make, you'll probably feel conflicted.

Let's say that you have an old friend who has just joined your office. Great! But what if he doesn't mesh well with the rest of your office mates? What if you perceive

A Question of Honesty

There's a new boss in the department, and Chris really wants to impress her with his analysis of a project completed in the last quarter. Chris has all the facts and statistics at hand, but he knows he's not a good writer. He's not good at putting it all together in a coherent way.

But Chris has a secret weapon. All the computers in the office are connected, and there's a shared hard drive on the system. Chris has access to all his coworkers' work. His friend Alicia writes sensational reports. She has already produced a summary of the last quarter's project for a different purpose for the previous boss. Chris sees no reason he shouldn't benefit from her good work. After all, they're a team, aren't they? And Alicia is done with that report.

So Chris prepares his report for the new boss, cribbing most of Alicia's original wording. He doesn't think he needs to mention this to Alicia. She wouldn't mind, and she's busy with other things now anyway.

After Chris submits his report, the new boss, Lindsay, calls him in for a little talk.

"I've seen this before," she says flatly. "This is Alicia's report."

Chris is dumbfounded. How could Lindsay have seen the report? It was submitted before she came on board. But when she was bringing herself up to speed, she must have read it. Of course!

"Well," he stammers, "It's not *all* Alicia's report. I mean, it's got some of the same information because it's about the same project. But the summary tables and the final sales data—I added that."

"Part of what I'm doing in this phase of getting to know the office," explains Lindsay, "is finding out the quality of people's work. So I gave *you* a report to do about last quarter's project, to describe it for me and provide a summary of objectives and accomplishments. That's not what this is. If I'd just wanted a table of data attached to Alicia's old report, which was completed before the project was completely over, that's what I would have asked for."

Chris shifts uncomfortably in his chair. "I'm sorry," he says. "I didn't understand."

"Does Alicia know you used her report?"

Chastened, Chris shakes his head.

"Well, this says a lot about you, Chris—and nothing good. I expect you to do your own work in the future and not steal anyone else's. And from now on, I'll be watching you closely." ■

that he gets a little jealous and hurt when you chat with another coworker, one whom he hasn't managed to befriend? This is an old friend; you don't want to let him down! On a personal level, he's more important than anyone else in the office. But then again, all your work relationships are important, and if one or two particular friendships demand all your social energy at the office, you will not be as comfortable with your other colleagues. This will translate to small obstructions in the flow of work-related communication.

Keep in mind that, strictly speaking, work is not the proper arena for your social life. At work, work concerns have to come first. If you see that a workplace friend-

66 99 **Advice for managers:** Supervising friends carefully.

Sometimes it's hard to maintain a balance between informality and authority with your team. Many managers befriend their employees, which is natural. This is especially true of managers who have been promoted internally and have previously established friendships. It is difficult to accept your change in status from peer to supervisor. You don't want to damage those friendships or start giving orders to your old buddies.

Many managers have trouble delegating work to, or imposing deadlines on, their friends. It's easy to fall into a vague, nondirective management style when you are close to the people you're supervising.

All the same, you have to find a way to keep your expectations clear and to fulfill your duties as a manager. If you have established personal friendships, you can leave the boss role behind at the office when you see them outside work. But challenging as it may be, you are responsible for discipline and accountability in your department. Some managers find this easier to do this if they maintain some emotional distance from their workers. You don't have to be cold, but you do need to be clear and consistent about your social and professional boundaries. Those boundaries may change over time. You must find your comfort zone and strike a balance that permits you to be an effective supervisor.

ship is distracting you from your job, talk to your friend about it after-hours or at lunch. Or arrange social events on weekends when you can look forward to conversing more freely.

Spouses at Work   Two people marry because they love each other and want to live happily ever after. They have mutual interests, so they decide to go into business together or to work for the same company. This is not an uncommon scenario, but is it a good idea?

Married or not, any two people involved in a romantic relationship must constantly build intimacy. It is vital to figure out how to be close, yet have space, or have space and yet feel close. Sara and Jack, for example, may not always crave closeness at the same time. In fact, Jack may want to be close at the very time Sara needs to pull back a little. Obviously there are times when things are congruent, but there are inevitably other times when partners are not on the same page, resulting in conflict. Combining these personal relationship dynamics with business can result in any number of emotional and logistical difficulties, not only for the couple but also for their coworkers. In a close-knit work environment, the "emotional weather" can spread quickly. Discord between married partners can be overbearing and distracting to others. Couples should take this into account if they decide to start a business and intend to hire employees.

If a couple has considered all of the ramifications and still wants to open their own business together, a productive first step would be to sit down with a piece of paper and draw up a grid of responsibilities. Write down what each person's role will be, what their compensation and profit desires are, and how much time they plan on dedicating to work on a daily or weekly basis. Add to that list a method for dispute resolution, because disputes *will* arise.

Similarly, whenever married partners work together at the same company, they should have a clear agreement about when (or if) they will interact during the workday. They should have well-defined boundaries about when it is all right to stop by each other's offices and how to behave with each other around coworkers. They should plan what times of day they will see each other or meet for lunch and which hours they will leave each other entirely alone.

Being in business together need not destroy a romantic relationship—or disrupt the flow of the workplace—as long as clear lines are drawn between work and home. Time must be allocated for personal time—no business chatter allowed! Just as importantly, personal issues must be left out of the workplace. A marital spat cannot be allowed to infect the next day's business activities. A couple should not allow their personal difficulties to bleed into the workplace. Simple as it may sound, this is a difficult balance for most couples to achieve.

Similarly, people who work with married couples must not permit marital strife to impinge on the emotional composure of the work environment. If necessary, someone may have to be blunt with the couple and let them know that their marital "issues" are a distraction in the office. Rules for when and how married partners should communicate during work hours may need to be imposed, or at least suggested, by third parties.

I would never advise a couple to work together; if they must, I would counsel against operating a business out of a home office. Nor would I recommend that couples be employed at the same office, especially if it's a small business. Large corporations tend to be easier, particularly when a couple works in two unrelated departments.

Short of parenting, marriage is the most complex, multifaceted, and demanding relationship there is. Working together just makes it that much more complicated. While I don't advocate it, melding the personal and professional is possible if you establish clear boundaries and are diligent about keeping them intact.

Attraction in the Workplace   While developing crushes and attractions in the workplace is not uncommon, it is extremely rocky terrain. Just as I advise against working with a spouse, I urge you to avoid dating coworkers. If you choose to do so, however, it is imperative to conduct yourself according to the following guidelines.

Sexual attraction *will* arise at work—this is normal. The proper arena to explore such attractions, though, is *not* the workplace. Be discreet. If the object of your affection is interested in you as well, find a way to meet outside the work environment. In addition to maintaining your professional image, you will also avoid prying eyes and gossip, which can place unnecessary stress on your budding romance.

Should you decide to pursue this relationship further after getting to know each other outside the workplace, it is imperative to refrain from any sort of touching or similar signs of affection in the office. This may sound obvious, but with sexual attraction, common sense often takes a back seat. Aside from the damage any sort of affectionate behavior may wreak upon your professional image, sexual harassment laws are always in effect in the office. Particularly when a relationship is new and you do not yet know each other's boundaries, you may be physically intrusive despite your best intentions. *Never*, under any circumstances, initiate or partake in any sort of intimate physical contact at work.

If you are in a supervisory role and are attracted to a supervisee, *just forget it*. Don't pursue it. Any word or deed that smacks of sexual innuendo can be easily construed—often rightfully so—as sexual harassment. While you may think you're receiving a favorable response, your worker may be scared of you or hoping to gain favor by leading you on. The potential for abuse of power goes both ways. What if your new lover starts to slack off at work? Will you treat this person in precisely the same way you would any other employee? Even if you are able to keep your professional relationship decorous, coworkers may perceive abuses of power on either side, resulting in great, potentially irreparable professional damage to both parties.

The Mentor Relationship

If you're very lucky, your boss is a mentor to you. This can be one of the healthiest, most productive relationships possible in a work environment.

A mentor cares about you, coaches you, and teaches you about things you need to know. He or she is someone for whom you feel trust, respect, and affection, a role model, someone whom you want to emulate.

In a work situation, a mentor-boss educates you about ways of advancing your career and provides opportunities for you to learn by experience. The mentor-boss takes an interest in you and your professional development. He helps you clarify your goals and introduces you to (or somehow assists you in meeting) the right people who can give you a leg up in achieving those goals.

Most of us have had mentors at some point. Maybe your favorite mentor was your mom or your dad, your track coach, your older cousin, or your ninth-grade English teacher. In any event, your mentor either recognized that you had a distinctive talent worth cultivating or was a kindred spirit. A mentor perceives something of value in you, something worth putting time and energy into, something worth coaxing into full bloom. Your mentor sees you as you would like to be seen—in the glory of your full potential.

Some brilliant bosses are mentors to their entire staff, but those bosses are rare indeed. Still, if you have an easy rapport with your boss, if you intuitively understand her and feel understood in turn, and if you respect your boss's judgment and wisdom, that is an excellent basis for a

Hiring Family

All too frequently, family and friends come looking for work, creating a delicate, pressure-filled situation. I received a typical cry for help from one of my radio show listeners, a fellow named Mike.

"My brother-in-law wants me to hire his son (my nephew) either part-time or full-time to work at my hardware store. My nephew has not worked since he dropped out of college in the spring. I would like to help since he is family, but I can't really afford a new employee, especially since I don't know if my nephew would be a good employee. He doesn't know that much about tools and paint and the things my customers would have questions about. Is it fair to offer to pay him less than the other employees? I pay the other employees about double the minimum wage since they all have been at my store a few years or more. I could really only pay my nephew seven dollars an hour or so. And if he is not a good worker, how can I fire him?"

I tell Mike, "Sit down with your brother-in-law, explain the situation and say, 'Hey, you know I'd like to help because it's family. On the other hand, I do see a problem because I have a business that's doing all right but I can't afford to make a lot of mistakes. Your son frankly doesn't have a great work ethic at this current stage in his life, and I don't want to be put in an uncomfortable position of paying him when I can't really afford another worker. Not to mention that I'd feel stuck with him and I couldn't fire him if he

didn't do a decent job.' Your brother-in-law ought to appreciate this honest answer. If he does not appreciate it, then you're in a no-win situation with him anyway."

Mike's in a tough situation here. Family is family, but it's usually not a good idea to mix it into the workplace—especially under these circumstances. Fortunately, Mike was able to find a good solution to the problem, one that at least for the present kept everyone satisfied.

FOLLOW-UP: A MONTH LATER

"We worked out a compromise," Mike told me some time later. "I spoke to my brother-in-law as you suggested, and I wound up offering my nephew a temporary job, a limited engagement of six months or so to see how things work out in the store. I've included a no-fault termination clause in the hiring agreement to protect myself, which means that the job is going to end on a schedule. So I'm not gonna be the bad guy at the next family Thanksgiving, after all!" ∎

mentor relationship. If all these pieces are in place, just give it time. Don't demand too much of her attention. Perhaps you can ask for advice once in a while, at appropriate times, when she is not distracted. As your boss begins to see how much you value her perspective, she might begin to fall naturally into a mentor role, which could have practical benefits for you and emotional benefits for both of you.

This *is* a special relationship—a kind of *favored* relationship, in fact—and in a work environment, you must handle your part of it delicately. Don't be obvious about this relationship. *Never* flaunt it to your coworkers; in fact, do the opposite. Downplay it and keep it as invisible as you can. Whatever you do, never act as if you expect special favors or privileges as a result of your status with the boss. This type of attitude is tantamount to a betrayal of the relationship, which in itself is an ongoing gift to you not a contract. Treat the relationship with respect, and do not take it for granted.

All It Really Takes

Despite the complexity of many of these issues, building successful, happy relationships at work ultimately comes down to a handful of simple actions and attitudes:

- Be polite and courteous.
- Give encouragement and praise.
- Listen to people.
- Be direct but not confrontational.
- Be collaborative, cooperative, and open.
- Build your achievements on teamwork.
- Have compassion for your fellow worker.

As John Kotter says in *Leading Change*, "Listening with an open mind, trying new things, reflecting honestly on successes and failures—none of this requires a high IQ, an MBA degree, or a privileged background."

Whether you are the boss or you have one, you have a responsibility to your organization, its mission, and its bottom line. Similarly, you also have a responsibility to maintain healthy personal relationships in the workplace.

Symptoms of a Healthy Working Environment

- People trust and respect each other.
- People take joy in each other's accomplishments.
- People encourage and support one another; coworkers are friendly without being "cliquish."
- People are honest about their feelings, without being discourteous.
- People are generous and fair about giving credit to one another.
- People are scrupulously honest and expect the same from others.
- Exceptional achievements are publicly recognized and rewarded.
- Romantic relationships are not flaunted in the workplace.
- People are able to listen well to each other.
- Everyone feels as though they have something important to offer, and that their contribution is appreciated.

conclusion

mental hygiene: working on yourself

The Foundation   This is the most important chapter in the book, because it's about the most significant working relationship in your life: your relationship with yourself. This relationship, your inner life, not only shapes how you feel moment by moment, it also determines how you perceive the external world, how well you function at work, and how your presence in the workplace impacts everyone else there. It all starts with a concept I call "mental hygiene."

The phrase *mental hygiene* first came into vogue about one hundred years ago, when a remarkable man named Clifford Beers wrote an autobiography entitled *A Mind That Found Itself.* His book described his experiences in the mental hospitals of the day, and he used the term *mental hygiene* to describe his personal methods of achieving sanity and clarity and of helping other mentally ill individuals heal. Around 1950 or so, the term *mental hygiene* gave way to *mental health*, which remains in our common vernacular today, both in professional and nonprofessional circles.

Reclaiming Cleanliness   I want to revive the term *mental hygiene* to define something other than an absence of clinical mental illness. *Hygiene* means health born of cleanliness. For our purposes, *mental hygiene* means the kind of health you maintain through purity of understanding. It means keeping your head and heart clear and open, free of impure thoughts. I refer here not to "immoral" thoughts but to

169

the kind of harmful thoughts that damage your sense of self-worth and self-confidence and your ability to succeed at work and get along with others.

People sometimes get hung up on words like *clean* and *pure*, as if someone is going to try to take away their sex life. But I want to reclaim the concepts of cleanliness and purity for ordinary folks who don't aspire to saintliness or celibacy. Just as your body feels refreshed when you take a shower, your spirit is happier when you keep your mind clean of negative garbage. This is not the psychological Olympics. It's simple and straightforward.

When I ask you to practice mental hygiene, I am referring to keeping yourself psychologically balanced, in tune with your surroundings, and adaptive to your circumstances. In a fast-paced, dynamic, changing work environment, mental hygiene is indispensable.

Please understand that mental hygiene is *not* about denying yourself the joy of life—just the opposite, in fact. It's about enjoying *more* inner freedom and lasting happiness.

The techniques that I'll cover in this chapter are as important for your mind as flossing and jogging are for your body. But just like cleaning your teeth and exercising your heart, taking charge of your mental hygiene requires some dedication.

Self-Awareness

Mental hygiene begins with self-awareness. What are you feeling right now? What's on your mind?

Most people believe that they are self-aware. But being self-aware is not a personality trait, it's an ongoing process. It's something you have to do moment by moment—"checking in" with your feelings. I don't mean driving yourself crazy, as in "How am I feeling now? And now? And now?" No, as I stated earlier, mental hygiene is not a strenuous or esoteric discipline, and neither is self-awareness.

Think of self-awareness as remembering to "touch base" with you. Especially when you are in a potentially stressful situation at work, remember to look inside for a moment. "What feelings am I having? What is my gut reaction to this person? Am I fearful? Ashamed? Guilty? *Why?*" This simple, easy habit will make you much less likely to "act out" in anger or defensiveness with your coworkers or to ascribe ignoble motives to colleagues without reflecting carefully on your evidence.

In addition to periodically checking in with yourself, the other dimension of self-awareness is simply *allowing a space for your emotions.* Allow your emotions to be what they are and accept them—even when they're not the most desirable emotions. It's the same with your thoughts. Don't judge your thoughts. Just notice them. This is self-awareness.

It's okay to be depressed, angry, fearful, anxious, guilty, or even ashamed, even though these emotions are not pleasant and we don't aim for them. In fact, the first step toward healing negative emotions is making a space for them when they arise, rather than judging yourself. Everybody gets the blues, everybody gets scared, and everybody gets a little twisted inside. With self-awareness, you begin to clear the space for more comfortable feelings.

Gut Feelings Like so many other people (perhaps even you), I was taught at a young age that I should rely on logic and verbal skills to cut through obstacles and get what I wanted. But as I gained experience and learned about myself, I begin to realize that my best counsel often comes from "the small voice inside," the voice that flows from my intuition, my unconscious mind.

Sometimes it's not even a voice, but a gut feeling. According to Daniel Goleman in *Working with Emotional Intelligence,* "The brain areas involved in gut feelings are far more ancient than the thin layers of the neocortex, the centers for rational thought that enfold the very top of the brain. Hunches start much deeper in the brain."

Timothy Wilson is a psychology professor at the University of Virginia. His interest in the role intuition plays in shaping our lives led him to write a book called *Strangers to Ourselves: Discovering the Adaptive Unconscious.* His tools can be applied to the workplace, allowing you to get in touch with and act upon the unconscious (or, put another way, your gut feelings) in a constructive way. I was fortunate enough to have him on my radio show, and he said:

"I think there's been a revolution in psychology in the last several years in how we view unconscious thinking. Unconscious thinking used to be viewed from a Freudian perspective in which it was this dark beast in the basement that everyone wanted to keep at bay and do their best to avoid thinking about. But the modern view is quite different. Actually a great deal of our mental processing occurs unconsciously, and it's a good thing that it does. We have very powerful brains that are able to size up the world, analyze it, and size up other people in ways that we don't even know we're doing. It's a very powerful way of perceiving and thinking about the world.

"I don't think that we can just stare inwards and suddenly the doors open and we have a direct view of our own unconscious processing anymore than we can stare at the wires of our computer and figure out what our computer's doing. We almost have to look at ourselves as an outsider would and watch what we do, watch our patterns of behavior, and try to deduce our own unconscious processing. That's not easy. But I think psychologists are realizing more and more that there's a part of our minds beneath the surface which is a smoothly running machine; we just don't have access to it directly."

Take a Step Back   The first step to making use of unconscious thinking is to make a kind of observational split within yourself, to step back and look at yourself objectively, to feel your emotions yet not be driven by them. It can take time to get the hang of this.

Wilson also suggests paying attention to what other people think. That doesn't mean automatically assuming that they're right and you're wrong about a situation or behavior, but if all of your friends and colleagues are observing more or less the same thing and giving you the same feedback, there is probably more than a grain of truth there. For example, if someone says, "You know, you seemed terribly uptight at today's staff meeting," then another coworker mentions the same thing, you might consider it—even if you don't remember feeling uptight at the meeting. Maybe you were making some unconscious gesture or your face had an expression that was broadcasting tension, and maybe you were stressed about something but didn't realize it.

The goal is not to adopt other people's views all the time, but to learn to intelligently question your thinking and not assume you are infallible. Oddly enough, paying attention to what your colleagues and friends tell you about yourself is another way of cutting through the chatter in your mind and getting in touch with what's real and what's happening in your emotional reality, as well as in theirs.

Those Negative Tapes

Much of maintaining good mental hygiene involves erasing the tapes that you listen to in your head. You know what I'm talking about: those tapes that tell you how you're supposed to act, what you're worth, how capable you are or aren't. The ones that remind you that you'll never get it, you're not good enough, you can't succeed . . . all that nonsense.

For example, I realized a long time ago that no matter how much success I had, whenever one deal fell through, it felt like I got kicked in the teeth. I had a tape recorder in my head that would play the same tape over and over.

"See, you've fouled things up again," it would say. "You think you're so good, but you're not." I spent so much time giving credence to those negative thoughts that I caused myself endless unnecessary suffering and wasted energy I could have focused on building my business. There may have been a grain of truth in what I was telling myself, but it was certainly not the whole picture. While honest and measured self-criticism has its place, be vigilant about avoiding incessant negative thinking.

Turn Off the Voices   If you are like most people, you have been listening to negative, critical tapes in your head for so long that they sound like your own voice. But they're not. They are the voices of others—parents, teachers, bosses—who have grafted their value systems, their standards of success and virtue, onto your life.

More than likely, those critics never meant to harm you. Unfortunately, though, it's too late for them to rerecord their messages. The things we convince ourselves of, the awful, self-hating tapes we play, can have significant detrimental effects on our vital energy and self-esteem and can wreak havoc on our ability to work with clarity and focus. The negative tapes compromise our capacity to maintain harmonious relationships with others inside and outside the workplace. You have to erase those old programs and replace them with new reality-based tapes.

Think of how you would feel about yourself at your job if your work was always criticized and nobody ever laughed at your jokes. Initially, you might think your coworkers were just jerks, but after a while you could very well internalize these messages and question your own validity.

Some work situations are oppressive, but there are very few that can make you feel crazier than being stuck inside your own head. Humans are complex creatures, and nearly a century after Freud, we are still, in many ways, just beginning to understand what really goes on inside our heads.

Replacing the Mental Tapes   Being aware of the bad tapes is one thing. Getting rid of them is another. So where do you start? Start by asking yourself: Is this really true? Why do I think this?

Whatever you do, don't get mad at your tapes. Don't scream, "Go away! I hate you! I will *not* think like this!" That just gives them more power. It is far more effective to be gentle. Acknowledge that these thoughts hurt. Ask yourself why that voice in your head would say such a thing. Does it have any basis in reality? Is it going to help you or clarify your life in any way to believe what this voice is saying?

Make a concerted effort to replace these negative self-perceptions with positive messages. Again, this is not a military exercise. Do it gently, in a way that works for you. Many people give themselves affirmations every day, positive phrases that they repeat to themselves many times or at various points—phrases like *I am a beautiful, kind, loving person. I am a success. I am competent and courageous.* For many people, affirmations make a tremendous difference in their internal environment and have a profound effect on their work life, too.

If affirmations fit your style, use them! Find ones that you like and that resonate with you and your needs.

At the very least, remember the successes and positive choices you make every day. Take stock of the value you contribute to your workplace. Put at least as much mental emphasis on your strong points as you do on your weak ones. Stop beating yourself up for every mistake you make. Stop interpreting your mistakes as proof that you're really a fake. Remember the old saw about learning from your mistakes and viewing each failure as an opportunity to try again and take a better path.

The Perils of Perfectionism

Perfectionism is a terrible disease of the mind and one that afflicts many of us. Perfectionism tells us that if we don't do things exactly right—if we don't score 100 percent on every test, if we don't meet all of our goals and expectations every day—then we've failed. Daniel Goleman notes in *Working with Emotional Intelligence* that for those who lack self-confidence, every failure confirms a sense of incompetence.

Who Wants Perfection?   Only dead or unborn people avoid all mistakes. It is essential to realize that your value as a person does not depend on success or failure. Rather, your worth is a function of your integrity, effort, and attitude.

Despite what the commercials and sports slogans say, life is not all about being number one. It's about hearing and following your own drummer and constantly applying your best effort with cheerfulness, humility, and consideration of your fellow human being. In a healthy workplace, mistakes are accepted as part of life. Think about it. Which kind of coworker do you appreciate more: the one who obsesses about never making a mistake or the one who is thoughtful and considerate and does her best?

Be proud of yourself for having the courage to take calculated risks. The greatest scientific discoveries in human history came about as a result of countless trials and errors. The greatest baseball hitter in history failed to get on base at least six out of every ten times he stepped up to the plate. The only real failure is giving up.

Perfection does not exist in the real world. It is an ideal, not an actual state. It is the point we are ever striving toward and ever approaching. If everything were perfect, things would come to a standstill. What would there be left to do? Be glad you're not perfect. Welcome to the human race, where we're all just blundering along, doing the best we can.

Worry   Excessive worry is poison to the mind. It's exhausting and detrimental to your physical and emotional health. Compulsive worrying fills the mind with frightening scenarios that need never come to pass. Worrying is paralyzing; in a

"Breaking the Tapes"

Georgia goes out to lunch with her friend and coworker Sandy. She tells her, "I've been feeling terrible anxiety at work lately. I just feel so guilty inside, like I don't deserve this job, and I don't deserve the respect of my coworkers."

"What do you mean, Georgia? Everybody likes you. You're a wonderful person and you do a terrific job."

"Yeah, but it's like I've got this voice of my mom in my head, telling me I'm no good, and sooner or later it's all going to fall apart and people are going to see through me."

"I see you perfectly clearly, Georgia," says Sandy. "I see a great woman who's been hard on herself her whole life. You suffer way too much! You don't have to, you know. I'm sorry your mom was mean but, I mean, isn't she dead now?"

Georgia chuckles ironically. "She's never dead inside me. It's like she controls my mind. I just *know* I'm going to make a big mistake sooner or later and get myself fired or get everyone mad at me or something."

"Your mother was just *wrong* about you. That's all there is to it," declares Sandy. "From now on, let *me* be in your head! When you hear your mom telling you all those terrible things, just look over at me, and know what I'm saying now. I know the *real* Georgia! I work with her every day, and I love her, and we're *lucky* to have her. Georgia is powerful and competent and beautiful and loved! Say that to yourself—or hear me saying it, because it's true."

When they go out to lunch a week or two later, Georgia tells Sandy, "Thanks so much for your words the other day. It's like I have a new ally in my head now, and I feel a lot better. Whenever I feel my mom's voice coming in, I just turn it over to you."

"And I kick her butt, don't I?" says Sandy, her eyes flashing triumphantly.

"Actually, you do a pretty good job," confirms Georgia. ∎

work situation, it makes you less, not more, effective and productive. Worst of all, worrying can be addictive. Like a rotten tooth you just can't resist irritating, worrying thoughts have an evil power of attraction.

Admittedly, worrying does have a few legitimate uses. It can alert you to danger and motivate you to prepare for the worst and to take the action necessary to counteract impending difficulties. More often, though, worry can steal your sleep, cloud your mind, confuse you, compromise your self-esteem, distract you from constructive thought, and make you anxious and depressed. Not a good bargain.

How to Beat the Worry Game

So what to do if you're a worrier? Here are some ideas. First, are your concerns rational? Some worries are reasonable, others are not. Can you tell the difference? If you have a stain on your shirt from lunch and you think your boss might see it, think you're slovenly, and lay you off next week out of sheer disgust, this is probably an irrational worry. On the other hand, if half your coworkers have been laid off during the past month, it makes sense to be concerned that you might be next.

If you decide that your worry is serious, make a plan to minimize its consequences. Also, look for a silver lining. If you lose your job, you might find a better one, and for the time being at least, you'll get a little more time to spend with your kids.

Ask yourself how much this concern is going to matter a year from now, or even next week. If the thing you're worrying about is something that, upon reflection, is not going to impact your life for very long, why not drop it?

If you really can't let go of a worry, sometimes it may help to vent. Talk to someone you trust, someone who may have the wisdom to put your worries in perspective. Choose listeners who care about you and have shown compassion.

Also, don't underestimate the importance of daily maintenance to your mental state. I mean the basics: Get enough sleep, meditate, stretch, walk, or pray. But *don't drink alcohol or take drugs to alleviate your worry*; ultimately that will backfire and you'll have more to worry about.

Give yourself credit for all your accomplishments and for all the resilience you've demonstrated. Remember how energized and optimistic you've felt at the best times. And while you're reflecting on your achievements, keep taking positive actions. Every proactive step you take will lessen the power of your worrying mind.

Some Common Negative Thinking Patterns

One of the most common negative mental traps is a false sense of helplessness, the sense that you have no power over a situation, that you are at the mercy of circumstances. This is almost never entirely true. Even in the direst circumstances, you have the power to make changes. Mental hygiene means rejecting (or at least questioning) thoughts of helplessness. Ask yourself, "What *can* I do here?"

Poor Me

Then there is something I call the *Poor Me* mindset. The mantra of the Poor Me archetype is "It isn't fair." Another term for this type of attitude is *playing the victim*. It's a lot like helpless thinking, but it also has a mildly resentful tone, which makes it more toxic. People who take this attitude are *always* unpopular at the office. No one likes to work around someone who feels sorry for herself all the time.

Self-pity is a trap. It's a do-nothing state of mind that drags you down, leaves you drained, and erodes your self-esteem. It's okay to feel a *bit* sad for yourself once in a while. You can cut yourself that much slack. But if you should ever happen to notice—when you check in on yourself and practice that self-awareness we were talking about earlier—that you're starting to *enjoy* the feeling of self-pity, watch out! You're in a danger zone. Snap out of it, and challenge yourself to do something positive.

Negative Time Warp

Then there's what I call the *Negative Time Warp*, the state of mind in which you cannot imagine that your

Getting Noticed

One recurring workplace complaint is that people don't feel adequately appreciated by their bosses, which causes them to worry. So maybe I get a call from someone who's feeling that way, and I try to explore the issue. If George is upset because his boss never notices all the good work he does, first I ask George how he wants to be noticed.

ME: So George, what would it look like, if your boss were to give you the attention and respect you deserve for all your fine work?

GEORGE: Well, it would be explicit, you know? Maybe an occasional thank you, or just . . . verbal acknowledgment of my work.

ME: Okay, so you want to hear it in words. You're doing a good job. Is that right?

GEORGE: Well, sure. Doesn't everybody need to hear that?

ME: Not necessarily. Do you feel picked on?

GEORGE: Huh?

ME: Do you feel that your boss is nasty to you, or thinks you're doing a bad job?

GEORGE: No, it's not like that. He's just . . . checked out. Like it doesn't matter what quality of work I produce.

ME: Is he checked out entirely? I mean, does he do his job? Or is his mind some-where else?

GEORGE: Well, I think he does what he has to do adequately, I guess.

ME: Well, I want to give you some home-work, George. Or actually, it's more like work-work. While you're at work, I want you to start noticing the specific ways that your boss talks to you, or doesn't talk to you, and what it is specifically that makes you feel underappreciated.

GEORGE: But I already told you that. It's that I'm not acknowledged for what I do.

ME: I know you told me that, George. But I want to know what your boss actually does do in relationship to you. I mean, does he ignore you altogether?

GEORGE: Um . . . no.

ME: Okay, then. Just pay close attention over the next week or so to your conver-sations with him, then call me back, and maybe we can examine this a little closer.

Sometimes our worries have a basis in reality. At other times, as in this example, there may be more to the matter. For George, the first thing was to find out if his worries about the boss's lack of attention were justified. That's why I told him to listen carefully to the con-versations he had with his boss. And those conversations, as well as George's other interactions at work, provided the necessary clue to understanding the real situation.

FOLLOW-UP: A WEEK LATER

So George called me back the next week and said, "I noticed that the boss doesn't really give anybody much appreciation."

ME: Oh, so you don't feel singled out for lack of appreciation anymore?

GEORGE: It's more than that. I get how he is. He's a low-key kind of guy. I'm plenty appreciated! I just didn't realize it.

ME: Oh good. So then he has *some* way of letting you know that? What is it?

GEORGE: Well, actually, I don't know if the boss appreciates me or not. I'm not altogether sure if big appreciation is part of his emotional repertoire, if you know what I mean. But I'm very appreciated by my coworkers. They give me all sorts of little strokes every day. I get smiles, I get friendliness, I get respect. I mean, I *feel* that moment by moment. There's always all these little cues, telling me I'm valuable and appreciated. They just don't come directly from the boss.

ME: But if the boss was *unhappy* with you, you'd know it?

GEORGE: I imagine so. But I don't even think about that so much anymore. I think up until now I've been conditioned to look to authority figures for approval, starting way back with my parents.

ME: Like most people.

GEORGE: Yeah, like most people, I guess. For me, bosses have always been like surrogate parents. I know that sounds weird, but in a way they're the ones who've provided for me; they're the ones who hold the purse strings. So I feel like I need to please them.

ME: Well, you do. That makes sense.

GEORGE: Yeah, but what I realize now is—I don't need to get emotional strokes from the boss. I get those from my coworkers. They're the ones who reflect my good work back at me in the way that they treat me. They're the ones who really reinforce my self-respect.

ME: Well then, you're a very lucky man, George. A lot of people feel competitive with their coworkers. It sounds like you've got some nice team spirit happening where you work.

GEORGE: Oh, there're some who are competitive, but not most. We all depend on each other, so it works out nicely. Maybe that's why we don't really need a boss who gets all involved with every little thing we do.

George figured out how to take care of himself and have his emotional needs met by looking in a different direction. This was superb mental hygiene on George's part. ∎

current troubles are ever going to go away or that things are ever going to get better. In your imagination, you're stuck in a permanent, unhappy present. You lose sight of the fact that no matter how badly it stinks, "this too shall pass." Step back and take a wider view. Things will change, whether you want them to or not. Every dark period of your life has a beginning and end, as has every glowing period. Accept that conditions will change, and take comfort in it. Life is an adventure, and there is no way of knowing what's down the road.

Finally, don't succumb to pessimism. It's easy to start believing all your negative thoughts and dismissing the positive ones. You can get to a point where you interpret everything through a negative filter. Say your boss praises your work. You might think, "Well, she's trying to make me feel better, but she's really not happy with me." Or your coworker is promoted, and you think, "Obviously, the boss thinks he does a better job than I do." In reality, though, your boss may be praising your work because you are a top-notch performer, and your coworker may have been promoted because he has six years' seniority over you.

So remember to notice the way you interpret events and other people's words. Be aware of your assumptions. Not everything that happens is a reflection on you. Often, you don't have all the information you need to draw accurate conclusions about other people's words and deeds. Keep an open mind, and expect good things. Be optimistic in your interpretations, and you'll find that other people respond well to your generous attitude.

The Impostor Syndrome   We spoke a couple of chapters ago about the Impostor Syndrome, when people feel false about what they do, as if they're getting away with a charade, though in reality they may be (and in most cases are) doing a genuinely fine job. The Impostor Syndrome is tied to two common fears: fear of failure and fear of success.

If you suffer from the Impostor Syndrome, it doesn't matter what external proof you may have of your accomplishments, what awards, academic degrees, job titles, or other recognition you've attained, or how much your boss and coworkers adore you. You still don't believe you've earned your success. It's always a matter of luck or good timing or having fooled everyone else into believing that you're smarter or better than you are—or so you believe.

You'd hardly think that people who have risen to the top of the corporate ladder would suffer from this syn-

66 99 | **Advice for managers:** Learn from your mistakes.

Everybody makes mistakes, even the best executives and managers in the world. In fact, their mistakes have probably made them even better at what they do in the long run.

It's not the mistakes you make but the way you recover from them that is the mark of a strong manager and an emotionally healthy person. Even Red Sox star Ted Williams only achieved a 0.344 lifetime batting average—that's not even four out of ten—and he was one of the greatest batters of all time. In some sales environments, especially the hard world of cold calling, a success rate of 10 percent is spectacular!

Of course, if you're in health care, your products had better be a lot more reliable than 50 percent. The CEO of a major automaker once quipped that if he built cars to the standards of most computers, the highways would be littered with cars and trucks that froze in place every now and then without any explanation and others that needed to be replaced after less than a year on the road. Definitions of acceptable error rates tend to be industry-specific.

All the same, if you never make a mistake, you never learn anything. And the biggest mistakes are the ones you can learn from the most. So I've got good news for you: You will make more mistakes in the future, plenty of them.

Executive intelligence means seeing your mistakes as opportunities—opportunities for a unique type of learning that can't be accomplished in any other way.

drome, but they do. In fact, people at all levels and in all professions can and do suffer from Impostor Syndrome. It leads to workaholism and what I call *compensatory self-esteem*, the frantic need to prove yourself without ever feeling as if you're actually able to do so.

The flip side is that if you succeed people will expect you to constantly deliver the goods, so you may sabotage your own success just to keep people from expecting too much.

This is how you can simultaneously be afraid of failing and afraid of succeeding. You work to excess, but don't allow yourself to feel successful.

There can be many reasons for Impostor Syndrome. It can be developmental, stemming from pressure you may have felt from your parents to get good grades in school. It can result from having been thrust into situations in which you were expected to do things that were beyond your training or ability. It may be that as a child you were consistently told that your efforts were "not good enough." The good news is that just as Impostor Syndrome and its related fears are self-inflicted, the cure can be self-administered.

Expand Your World   Often you can deal with these fears by expanding your horizons, spending more time in places where you're challenged creatively and even physically. If you enjoy sports, that can be a good place to start. Look for anything that will distract you from your obsessive, single-minded focus on high achievement. Taking some time off from work can be good. If that's not possible, see if you can be assigned to an unfamiliar project or task for a change, one that no one expects you to master off the bat.

Ask yourself what you are afraid of. Exposure? As hard as you've been trying to hide your "secret incompetence," such exposure might even be a relief. Or are you afraid of being successful? What does success entail? Will you have to live up to a high standard forever? Will people's expectations of you be too demanding and unrealistic? Will they be mad at you if you don't meet those expectations?

Well, let them be disappointed then. People are disappointed every day, and then they get over it. Your loved ones will not stop loving you, and your employer probably won't stop appreciating you either. Everybody else is probably giving you a lot more leeway than you're giving yourself.

Coping with Stress

No matter how healthy your self-esteem and how diligent your mental hygiene, you cannot avoid stress at work and in life. In one sense, stress keeps you toned. If you had nothing pulling on you, nothing straining you, you'd turn to flab inside and out. Stress is simply the pressure of demands from your environment. Sometimes those demands are too many or even contradictory. That's when stress is most overwhelming.

Stress is possible in any situation, and who doesn't feel work-related stress? But though we should never expect a completely stress-free life, we should try to moderate our stress, because excessive stress is unhealthy and unpleasant.

It helps to understand that there are two categories of stress: positive and negative. Positive stress is related to challenges you must stretch to meet. For example, being assigned a big work project to complete in a short time creates a positive (though substantial) stress. Ultimately, the outcome depends on you and your actions, your self-discipline, and your willingness to step up to the plate. Positive stress can also sometimes be found where you don't expect it, such as in conflicts at work, which you have the ability to resolve and to learn from.

Negative stress, on the other hand, arises from conditions over which you have little or no control. Negative stress can make you feel trapped. Such stresses include the loss of a loved one, a seemingly irreconcilable personality conflict at home or at work, or a severe financial crisis that feels insurmountable. But a strong-willed person can often transform negative stress into positive stress.

The personal repercussions of events such as stock market crashes, recessions, and outsourcing can stress you at least as much as anything or anyone in your office. More than localized conflicts with managers or coworkers, global circumstances that affect you directly but that are driven by events in the world economy may pierce you with feelings of powerlessness. Corporate scandals, mergers and layoffs, swings in the economy, and other factors in the world outside the office will impact your feelings at work and your relationships with coworkers. Uncertainty about the future or the general job climate is an enormous negative stress.

You're in Charge   While you cannot control these outside forces, you can take charge of your emotions, which will in turn greatly improve your ability to handle the negative stresses and survive the turbulent economy. To quote an old axiom: Tough times don't last, but tough people do.

As always, start with the basics. Keep eating a balanced diet and get plenty of sleep. In the short term, it might feel comforting to amp yourself up with a lot of coffee and sweets (or, worse yet, numb yourself with narcotics or alcohol), or to stay up late and throw your rhythms out of whack, but ultimately you'll deal with your challenges best by keeping your body nourished and your feet on the ground. In the end you'll also be less anxious, less jerked around by your stress. As Mitch Thrower counsels in *The Attention-Deficit Workplace*, "Your workplace cannot guarantee that you eat the right foods, so it's up to you to make sure that you do."

Don't let negative stress dictate the rhythm of your life. Keep putting one foot in front of the other, taking care of one item of business at a time. Sometimes you may have to push yourself a little, but avoid frenetic activity. Make a plan and pace yourself.

It is imperative to take breaks and get the relaxation and recreation you need during stressful times. You may feel as though you have no time to waste, but no regenerative activity is wasted. It will help you function better later, when you're plugging away at work. So schedule a little pleasure and relaxation every day.

Get regular exercise and, if at all possible, regular affection. Research has shown that people who are touched and loved live longer and healthier lives. Let yourself be nurtured by your significant other, and don't be afraid to ask to be touched and held when you need it (though work is not the place for this!).

Finally, as always, turn to your friends. Listen to them, and speak openly with them about your stresses. Ask them for advice. They may have answers that you might not have imagined. However, even if your friends cannot provide solutions to your negative stresses, they can soothe you just by listening to you, and alleviate the feeling of isolation that often accompanies stressful periods. Coworkers may also do this for one another.

Reducing Work-a-Day Stress

Even if you love your job, just going to work each day can be stressful. Chances are, on some days, you can think of a few places you'd rather be. Here are some tips for reducing the stress of daily work life:

- Take a few minutes in the morning to sit quietly and notice the sounds of your neighborhood, and the view from your window. Breathe deeply.
- Continue to take deep breaths all day long. While you're at your desk, take deep relaxing breaths whenever you think of it. Direct your awareness to the places in your body where you feel tense, and try and breathe out all that tension. Stand up, shake your arms out, flex your fingers, and stretch.
- Pack yourself a really nice lunch, try different restaurants, or go to a quiet park near work to eat your lunch. Make

breaks and lunchtime something to anticipate. Bring an interesting book with you to work, and read a few pages when you take short breaks. This will bring your mind to an altogether different place.

- If it feels natural and not too contrived, surprise your coworkers now and again with little gifts that they'll appreciate. These can be individual gifts, or things like fresh fruit to share with the entire crew. Don't make a big production of it; just offer something pleasant once in a while. It will brighten their day and yours too, and random generosity may even become a workplace norm. Small acts of kindness certainly mitigate everyone's stress, and increase the general sense of collective well-being.

- Finally, when you get home from work, change your clothes right away. Get comfortable. Wash your face and hands. If you come home to a spouse and/or family, ask about their day—it will refresh your mind to hear their stories.

Depression   The word *depression* is thrown around pretty carelessly these days and is used in a variety of contexts. Some people are depressed for years on end. This is called clinical depression and is a mental illness. Other people become temporarily depressed in response to specific circumstances or events. This is also a variety of depression, although arguably not as severe as the clinical variety. Classic signs of depression include insomnia or excessive sleeping, loss of appetite, loss of sex drive, feelings of helplessness and hopelessness, suicidal fantasies, listlessness, low energy, lack of interest in friends and recreational activities, and feelings of poor self-esteem.

If you are experiencing these symptoms and feel that you may be suffering from depression, don't criticize or judge yourself. It doesn't mean you are weak or defective. It indicates that you are experiencing an intense emotional challenge. Have some compassion for yourself. If you're not sure *why* you're depressed, don't worry about that too much either. The point is not to understand depression so much as it is to overcome it.

What if your best friend or favorite coworker was depressed? How would you treat that person? See yourself as that person.

Get busy! It has been clinically proven that one of the best ways to counteract depression is activity, even if the relief is only temporary. Rather than infecting others at your workplace with a mood of gloom (which, unfortunately, can happen when you're depressed), try to delve into your work. Jump-start yourself into a better mood through constructive action. Force yourself if you have to, but be productive!

Work out. Move your body. Break a sweat. Breathe fresh air deeply. To some extent, depression is physiological, and it can sometimes be dislodged by aerobic exercise.

No matter how unappealing the idea may be, force yourself to socialize. Go out to lunch with coworkers. Do not isolate yourself. If you can't stand socializing for more than thirty minutes, fine. Go visit a friend for half an hour. Even if you don't think you'll be able to appreciate his companionship, his life energy and warmth will seep through your skin, and it will help alleviate your depression.

If you don't feel like talking to anyone, write your feelings down. Even if you never show anyone else what you've written, getting your thoughts down on paper is therapeutic. Finally, remember that your depression is not the whole story. When you are depressed, you are not really seeing yourself or your world through a clear lens. Try to remember that sooner or later there will come a time when you are no longer depressed, and life will look very different.

Anger Without question, anger is one of the more difficult emotions. Of all the negative emotions, what makes anger so dangerous is that it's easy to feel *righteous* when you're in its grip. That can cause you to behave in nasty ways you may well regret after you've had a chance to cool off and reflect.

Let's face it: It's normal to get angry at work. However, there are productive and counterproductive ways to express this anger. Don't let anger rule you. A good way to deal with workplace anger is to allow yourself to feel and acknowledge it but not to automatically act on it. First, determine a way to channel your anger properly. This will act as a circuit breaker between your feelings of anger and your actions, ensuring that you remain in control and don't terrorize your coworkers!

Try to evaluate what happened to make you angry in the first place. Sometimes, anger is an unconscious reaction to personal events in the past and not necessarily related to something that just happened. Be sure to stop for a minute and ask yourself if you are making any assumptions about the situation that might not be true.

If you feel that you have a legitimate gripe, talk to your boss or coworker. Do not attempt to squelch your anger. If you try to suppress your anger, you're training yourself not to feel your feelings, which is dreadful mental hygiene. Before long you will start to *somatize*, or experience physical symptoms, like headaches, migraines, and high blood pressure.

When you state what you're angry about, avoid blaming your coworker. Concentrate on how you feel, and what's bothering you. Whatever you do, don't forget to *listen*. Allow your coworker to respond, and really hear his or her point of view. You may have been missing something important when you got angry.

If the other person starts to blame *you*, which in turn makes you even angrier, it is probably best to step out of the room for the moment and address the issue later. Research has shown that when people are having a heated argument, a simple cool-down period of twenty-five minutes or so allows their heads to clear enough to tackle the issue from a much calmer and less charged perspective. Even if the other person is the boss in this case, you can say, "I'm sorry. I need to stop talking about this now. I'd like to come back later and finish this discussion."

If you get angry a lot, it could be something you carry around inside, a painful memory or disappointment that really has nothing to do with the people in your work environment. This is a good occasion to exercise self-awareness.

What if no one did anything to upset you, but you find yourself feeling angry anyway? Pay close attention to your thoughts. Remember, sometimes, simple awareness heals and cleans the mind.

Burnout Burnout is one of my least favorite subjects because it's such a tragedy and so avoidable if people would only employ more self-awareness. Burnout is when you reach the point at which you can't even summon the energy and concentration you need to do your job. You've been working too hard for too long, perhaps for too little pay, and you've lost your enthusiasm. Your dreams, goals, and ambitions don't seem worth the effort anymore. Burnout is much more easily avoided than cured, but the prescription for avoidance and recovery are the same, and it's all based on common sense.

Take breaks when you need them and vacations when you can afford them. Spend more time with your loved ones, and get the emotional support you need from other people in your life. Get more rest. Be aware of how you're driving yourself, and ease your foot off the gas pedal. Look at what's causing you to burn out. What are the stressors in your daily life? Is all the pressure really coming from your boss or coworkers? Or is a lot of it coming from *you*?

If necessary, reframe your life goals, and consider a job change. Do whatever you have to do to rejuvenate, because burnout is terrible, and nothing—certainly not a job—is worth it. To some extent, your life energy is a renewable resource but not indefinitely. Take good care of it. Practice vital energy ecology as part of your mental hygiene regimen.

Nurturing Yourself: A Review of the Basics

Another, more touchy-feely term for mental hygiene is *self-nurturing*. Touchy-feely is not my style, but it is useful to call something what it is. As a baby, you are physically and emotionally nurtured by your mother. But as an adult, you have to take care of your basic needs. You have to be your own nurturer—or, more accurately, you have to manage your own nurture. You have to make sure your needs are being met, because nobody else is going to watch you at all times to make sure that your choices are healthy.

Maintain Physical and Mental Well-Being

Though part of keeping up your mental hygiene comes from self-awareness, the rest comes from your interactions with the other people in your life. So—no matter how angry, disappointed, or disillusioned you become—never cut yourself off from friends and family. People close to you can often provide the reality check you need to see where you're at and bring light to those things you can't see for yourself when you're too close to the situation. All too often, people hear concerns expressed by their family and friends and say, "No, no, I'm fine!" As your Business Shrink, I advise you to listen to your friends. Sometimes they know you better than you know yourself.

Then there's the physical side of mental hygiene. You learned this in kindergarten: Start the day with a decent breakfast, or at least something more nourishing than three cups of java. Showing up at the office hyped on caffeine is not the best route to problem-solving, clarity of mind, or easy relationships. It's also critical to make time for a regular exercise routine, no matter how busy you are.

Dr. Sidney Harman of Harman International, whom we met in the first chapter, once offered this business advice: "Never miss a day's physical workout." He was eighty-six when he said that and still began each day with an hour of aggressive tennis.

I have a colleague who gets out on the water every day he is home and rows for an hour. Aside from exercise, rowing also provides him with time to meditate and strategize; not coincidentally, this is when he conceives some of his most creative ideas. That workout is a consciously integrated part of his business life, and he makes every effort to leave his mobile phone onshore. Physical and mental health are intertwined, so exercise is *critical* to your mental hygiene.

When work gets too crazy and you become overwhelmed, slow down. A radical concept, I know. A friend first heard that advice as a teenager, while working in a restaurant. He was a busboy and dishwasher, and during one particularly crazy dinner hour (after the restaurant had received a favorable review in the local newspaper), the manager took him aside, put his hand on the boy's shoulder, and said, "Listen. When it gets really *really* busy around here, *slow down.*" He wasn't kidding. The manager knew a good employee when he saw one, and he didn't want my friend to burn himself out.

As a rule, slowing down is healthy and inexpensive. And yes, you do have time to slow down, no matter what our culture tells you. Slowing down is empowering. Slowing down is sane. Slowing down makes you more efficient in the long run. Knowing when to slow down is quintessential mental hygiene.

Journal Writing   One last self-nurturing technique I'd recommend is journal writing. While I know this is the ultimate touchy-feely sensitive thing to do these days, it also works. Like all transformational therapies or traditions, journal writing allows you to evaluate your own experiences—maybe not objectively but with some clarity. Believe it or not, it's been demonstrated in clinical tests that journal writing can actually cause physical healing, and anybody who's kept a journal knows how much good it can do you just to get things down on paper. Somehow it seems to get your problems and preoccupations out of your head, where all they do is drive you crazy. Journal writing also helps you to understand yourself, to get your needs and your goals and your feelings into clearer focus. It's an excellent self-awareness tool.

Hold Tightly to Your Values

The final foundation of mental hygiene is staying true to your values. As Peter F. Drucker said in his book *Management Challenges for the 21st Century*, "To be able to manage oneself, one finally has to know: 'What are my values?'" Nothing can wreak havoc with your peace of mind more than making moral compromises for the sake of short-term gain. It can be easy to do, and sometimes it may not seem like a big deal. There are a million ways it can happen.

For example, it might transpire, for one reason or another, that your boss believes a mistake you made was really someone else's fault. You didn't lie about it, but somehow, your boss got the wrong impression. To top it off, your coworker doesn't even realize what has happened. Would it be lying to let matters stand, without correcting your boss's perception?

Yes. You owe it to your boss and to your coworker to set the record straight. More than this, you owe it to yourself, because honesty is the key to your sense of self-worth and your abiding mental hygiene. More than this, down the road, your candor may have unexpectedly beneficial ramifications for your career, as people recognize just how much they can depend on your integrity. It's a very powerful thing to be seen as one who always tells the truth. It gives your word a lot of power.

Or maybe the temptation is about something that seems to have little importance. Your coworker comes to

you with a bit of malicious gossip about a colleague. What
do you do? Do you laugh and let it slide? Do you turn
away? Or do you respectfully defend the absent coworker
and ask the gossiping person to please not talk this way
about the other person with you? You don't have to be
sanctimonious about it; you can just say, from your heart,
"Hey, I don't like talking about her like this. It feels disrespectful, and I wouldn't want anybody talking about *me*
this way. Let's change the subject. What do you say?"

All these actions and interactions matter tremendously.
They all reflect your values. The happiest, most successful
people in life are the ones who are clear on what their
values are and who live consistently by those values in big
and small ways.

Recognize the
Perils of Unethical
Behavior

Certainly there are many cases of ferociously sick-in-
the-head business managers and owners who are successful in making money for their companies and for
themselves. But is that really success? What goes around
will eventually come around. I believe that the greedy,
selfish, unscrupulous captains of industry and commerce
are never happy. By definition, greed can never be completely satisfied. Yes, unethical businessmen may get rich,
but look at their pictures in the paper. When they smile,
does it look real, or does it chill you to the bone?

Recent corporate scandals underscore the critical importance of good mental hygiene. Take Ken Lay
and Jeffrey Skilling of Enron, for instance. Ken Lay died
before his time of a heart attack that was probably stress-
induced. Skilling is serving a twenty-four-year prison sentence. What game did they win exactly? Were they happy
when they were on top? I wonder. Lay, Skilling, and other
white-collar criminals who have fleeced their companies
of millions and left pensioners and stockholders without
a penny are textbook examples of failed mental hygiene.
They probably held strong values at one time and had
marvelous ideals and dreams of creating a great company

for themselves and everyone associated with it, but somewhere they got lost in the game of getting ahead.

They have paid a terrible price for neglecting their mental hygiene. They apparently don't know, or have lost sight of, the difference between right and wrong. They treat other people as objects and take liberties at the expense of others. True, some people do very well that way in the marketplace. But if this success comes at the price of their soul, if they see no greater meaning to life than leaving the Monopoly game with the most paper money and hotels, and they can't begin to even think about how what they do affects their fellow human being—then, no matter how much money they have accumulated, they are fundamentally bankrupt and decrepit. Never envy such people. They need help. Sadly, few of them get it.

By all means, aspire to great things. Become rich and famous! The world is your oyster. Just make sure to keep your body healthy and your mind clean, or you won't be able to enjoy the fruits of your life's labor.

Elements of Mental Hygiene

- Be self-aware of your thoughts and feelings, moment by moment.
- Pay attention to your gut feelings about people and situations.
- Replace the negative message tapes in your head with affirmations and positive messages.
- Learn from your mistakes instead of demanding perfection from yourself.
- Nurture yourself with good food and exercise.
- Minimize stress and avoid burnout by taking breaks when you need them.
- Make sure that your actions and words are consistent with your own most deeply held values.
- Turn to trusted friends and coworkers for support when you need it, and take their feedback seriously.

appendix

Following are excerpts from Peter Morris's interviews with the
Business Shrink's guests who are cited in the text of this book.

THE dysfunctional WORKPLACE

Peter Morris, the Business Shrink, talks to colleagues:

Caitlin Friedman »

Author of *The Girl's Guide to Being a Boss (Without Being a Bitch)*

PETER MORRIS: When did you first become a boss?

CAITLIN FRIEDMAN: Oh, it was a while ago. I had my first employee when I was a manager at a publishing company here in New York. And, you know, leading is tough. It's really hard to be a good manager.

PM: Did you feel that you were too tough or not tough enough?

CF: You know, I actually had a lot of the very common problems that women have in leadership positions. I was really afraid to delegate, and I became kind of a micromanager; I didn't really trust my employee to get the job done. I'm sure you guys have talked about this on the show before but there's something that's called the imposter syndrome. A lot of women, especially in leadership positions, suffer from this and they feel like they're . . .

PM: Not worthy.

CF: Yeah, unworthy, and they're faking it and their success is just because of good luck and not hard work. I had a lot of feelings like that, especially when I was delegating to someone. But eventually I kind of worked through it, and now as a business owner I have a team of five people, and I'm definitely more comfortable in that role. But it's not easy.

PM: No, it's not. And I'm here to tell you that the imposter syndrome is not gender specific. I've had that all my life in varying degrees, and it's very difficult. It gives you a fear, a great fear, of success and a fear of failure.

Most women, a survey has shown, would rather work for a man than a woman. Why do you think that is?

CF: Well, unfortunately, there's a lot of bad women bosses out there. They're judged differently and often unfairly. And a lot of women feel like there was an emotional expectation that their employee had of them. There isn't that expectation from a male boss.

Employees expected their women bosses to be more understanding and more conscious of work/life issues and engaged in a friendship level that makes it very difficult when you're a manager.

PM: So if they work for a man they don't have those same issues generally?

CF: No, they don't. And when it's working, that kind of level of relationship-building creates a great loyalty among a team with their manager. But on a bad day or when a female boss needs to discipline someone, it gets really rocky really quickly.

PM: What about the dynamic that I hear about—how women can be very catty and have sharp elbows and being competitive with each other in a less direct way; whereas men can bond and be buddies—when they have to be adversaries, they are, but there's more of a demarcation?

CF: That's interesting. I do think that that does happen. I think that women are socialized differently than men, and it comes out in the workplace. But we really believe that when women start addressing these confidence issues, when it comes to their management and leadership styles, a lot of that will go away.

We found that women tend to micromanage, because we're used to juggling a lot of home and a lot of work, we're used to having a lot on the plate. But what happens—when you start micromanaging—is that you're not empowering your team. When you disempower your team they're less energized to work for you. So you absolutely need to delegate.

The second thing, which is really a common issue, is that women tend to befriend their employees. They want, they really want, to be liked. So they are very uncomfortable delegating and they are uncomfortable disciplining. It erodes any sort of respect that they need to gain from their team.

We were talking before about the confidence issues. If you're insecure in your role as a boss then you tend to be a bit vague. Women are often uncomfortable delegating, so instead of saying, "This report is due on Thursday at nine," they'll say, "Well, if you could get that report done by next week that would be great." That's not really being clear, and that's not really helping your employee out.

PM: And that's a very good lesson. We can go back in the cinema world, and we have examples of bitchy bosses. I guess the latest one is Meryl Streep in *The Devil Wears Prada*.

CF: Yes. So she was . . . well, she was really interesting because she was kind of an old-school, stereotypical bad female boss. I mean, here was a character who had clawed her way through the ranks in a really competitive and very bitchy world of fashion and didn't support the women or even the men around her and didn't appreciate and support other people's success. Again, I do think that was a stereotype. I do think that that kind of leadership is kind of going away as people learn a bit more about how to do this correctly.

Gary Topchik»

Author of *Managing Workplace Negativity*

GARY TOPCHIK: Hello, Peter.

PETER MORRIS: Hello, Gary, how are you?

GT: Good. Hopefully, you're in a positive attitude today.

PM: I'm trying, and I think I am.

GT: Good.

PM: I've noticed from your bio that you've handled some very exalted companies: Shell Oil and Oracle and Southern Edison, AT&T, Fannie Mae, Dow Jones, Disney. A lot of outsiders would think, well, those guys should be pretty happy.

GT: The key to avoiding negativity or avoiding disgruntled employees, as many as these companies realize, is to keep building a positive work environment. So if you're proactive about it you can avoid a lot of the negativity. A big part of my business is to help companies build a more positive work environment.

PM: So what is a positive environment that avoids negativity?

GT: Simplistically it's the kind of environment where the vast majority of people feel motivated. They feel motivated either by their managers who manage them or by the learning opportunities, by the growth opportunities, or by the actual nature of the work that they do.

PM: And interestingly, although money is important I understand it's not the most important. A lot of the work environment that generates contentment and excitement relates to collaboration, cooperation, teamwork, and a sense of order.

GT: I think you're definitely right, Peter. In the States, at least, according to many, many studies, money does not seem to be on the top of the list of what motivates people at work. Most people, when they come to the workplace, expect a reasonable kind of salary for the kind of work that they do. But the salary itself is not what really motivates people. I think, as you were saying, it's the decision-making ability, it's the collaboration, it's having people ask you what you think. Plus, I think the biggest motivator for most people in today's workplace is the learning environment, where one can come to work every day and feel that they're learning or they're growing or they're developing their skills.

PM: Negative activities relate to bad-mouthing ideas, whining, sarcasm, frowning, people who want to bully other people and are dictatorial.

GT: Yeah. I think what causes people to become negative in a workplace are a few things. One, there are some people who come to the workplace and they're already in their negative mood. They have what we call a negative personality. And they're the ones who really start to spread the negativity. But even if you're the most positive person in the world and you come to the workplace, there are things that happen there that could cause you to become negative: no growth opportunities, having a bad manager, not having clear goals, clear directions. Maybe it's just a wrong job fit; maybe you should never have been in that job in the first place.

PM: Now how do we turn negative into positive?

GT: I treat negativity as a behavior problem. I think the first thing that has to be done is the person has to be told about their attitude. They have to be told that when you say this you're expressing negativity, or when you do this, or even the expression on your face. We've got to get that specific. Then tell them what they need to do instead.

PM: What are some of the techniques? Give us a few.

GT: I think venting is a great strategy. If you could find yourself a buddy in the workplace, someone you can go to and say, "Boy, she's doing it again!" "He's up to it again!" And really be able to spill your guts. That's a great little strategy. I encourage managers to have a time limit for negativity. For example you could say, "The first five minutes of our meeting just tell me what's going wrong. That's quite okay. But when 9:05 hits, we're going to talk solutions."

Something else that you can do, take a little time out. Go get a cup of coffee. Go walk around the block. Go walk around the building. Come back in ten minutes. It doesn't seem as bad as it used to.

PM: Gary, what do you do when you have a disgruntled or troublesome employee? How do you handle it?

GT: I think the first thing that a manager or a company has to do is to really try to provide a positive work environment. Try to find the motivators that would work for the person. Try to have good working conditions, good salaries, all that kind of stuff. If you do all that, chances are you're going to have much fewer disgruntled or demotivated people. But on the other hand, if you still have people who are disgruntled or demotivated and it begins to impact their own work or the work of others, then as I said before you really have to hold that person accountable and say, "Uh-uh, this behavior's not gonna go over. This is what I need for you to do instead." It's almost similar to having an employee who's late all the time or absent all the time or spreading rumors. You've got to treat it really the same kind of way.

PM: And, of course, holding the employee accountable, eventually the employee has to shape up or ship out.

GT: I would think so. Negativity is like a virus; one person has it, and before you know it they're spreading it around, especially if the other people are open to it. If their "immune system" is down, they're going to catch that negativity. And the worst person or the worst people to be negative are the people in leadership positions in the organization because they spread the negativity faster than any employee could possibly spread it.

PM: What can a leader do to pull out of that kind of a tailspin?

GT: Well, the first thing that has to happen is that somebody has to give the leader the feedback that they're actually coming across in a negative of way. Really make it a business issue. Say, "When you walk around saying, 'They don't know what they're doing upstairs,' it's really impacting the success of the organization. It's impacting productivity. It's impacting morale in the workplace, which is all very bottom-line kind of figures." Once we explain it to them in dollars and cents, that gets them to change their attitude more than anything else.

Justin Menkes »

Author of *Executive Intelligence*

PETER MORRIS: I'm fascinated with what you do and what you've written about. Please tell the audience.

JUSTIN MENKES: Just about for as long as anybody's been in business, we've all wondered what this facility some people have, this business acumen, this sharp common sense, that allows some people to do so well and others to be so hopeless. That's what *Executive Intelligence* is all about. It's clarifying what we mean by business acumen. What makes somebody a sharp business executive.

PM: And what *does* make somebody a sharp business executive?

JM: It turns out that it's a set of cognitive skills that they all have in common. It's like when you look at an exceptional basketball player; what differentiates Michael Jordan from his competitors, what made him so much better? Better, faster footsteps, better jumping ability: These are the things that made him so much more effective across any basketball situation. Similarly there's certain skills that make certain people better across any business situation: Evaluating the data you have in front of you, what do you know, what more do you need to know in order to make a sound conclusion?

PM: What else? What are the other cognitive skills that make for a good executive, for having executive intelligence?

JM: Interpersonal realms will make somebody a sharp, socially savvy, politically savvy, executive. Things like understanding issues from multiple perspectives. Being able to dissect things, understand underlying agendas. What's being said and what's being really meant by what's being said?

PM: Do you think emotional intelligence plays a big role in defining executive intelligence?

JM: *Emotional intelligence* is a term that has been used very broadly. If you define it as the ability to see things from multiple perspectives, the ability to understand complex interpersonal situations and understand the likely emotional reactions, these are the cognitive abilities that make somebody sharper with other people and if that is emotional intelligence.

PM: And tell us now what you do to apply this? Because you have been in the executive search business, as I understand, at Spencer Stuart and now you run a group that relates to executive intelligence called the Executive Intelligence Group. What does that do?

JM: We have an exclusive partnership with Spencer Stuart. We evaluate senior-level executives. And what we're talking about with executive intelligence is making explicit what the most effective star leaders have? Jack Welch, Sam Walton from Wal-Mart, they all had these exceptional facilities for the skills we're talking about. So what we do is measure those skills. In the book I show how you can do that.

PM: Three key categories are the ability to define a problem and prioritize, to recognize underlying agendas, and to understand your own mistakes and your own behavior. Those would seem to be critical prerequisites to being effective as a leader and as an executive.

JM: Absolutely. That's why we bring them up as all part of executive intelligence. You can't possibly execute a strategy effectively if you don't understand how to do so through other people. And you certainly can't execute strategy effectively or make a good decision if along the way you can't recognize when you're making a mistake, critically evaluate, and adjust and adapt.

PM: How do you learn these skills if you don't have them?

JM: The book has a lot of examples of some of the great decision-makers throughout time and interviews with many of those people. From those stories I create exercises you can use to practice skills.

PM: Can you give me some examples?

JM: Sure. Say an employee who is much lower down in your company than you comes to you and says her boss, who reports directly to you, is doing something terrible with a customer and she felt it was her responsibility to go over his head and go to you. How do you handle a circumstance like that?

You have to understand whatever you choose to do there are certain pitfalls here—for instance, disrupting the chain of command. You might upset the boss. You have to be very careful with how you handle the information. You have to find out what the problem is. Why this individual chose to go around the chain of command? These are some of the cognitive skills you would want to demonstrate as they you down these complex situations.

PM: To understand the dynamics.

JM: Absolutely. One of the things I talk about in the book is how the human brain is wired to jump to instant conclusions. That process made us survive in an environment with constant physical threats. We had no time to think. But in a complex business environment, that instant knee-jerk reaction can get us into trouble. Skilled executives take a moment or two to ask the right questions. Probe a bit. Because often a situation may appear to be one thing but in actuality it's something else. That's one of the reasons why executive intelligence is so rare. It's actually quite unnatural to take that sort of critical-thinking approach about yourself, about other people.

PM: Are there any other seemingly contradictory dynamics or dances that have to be mastered to become a star?

JM: Absolutely. Many senior executives as they move up the ladder find it more and more difficult to hear critical feedback or constructive criticism and use that construction criticism to arrive at a better answer. They begin to build a sort of yes-man or -woman team around them because they don't want to hear critical feedback when they think someone thinks they're wrong or are missing something. But that is a quality that we absolutely must fight. And in *Executive Intelligence* there are specific skills that enable you to keep using the great minds around you to arrive at a better conclusion.

Katherine Crowley》

Author of *Working With You Is Killing Me*

PETER MORRIS: Would you share the premise of your book with us?

KATHERINE CROWLEY: The premise of *Working With You Is Killing Me* is that work—the actual doing of one's job—is often relatively simple. The far more challenging thing about work is the relationships; the people you have to work with, the people who may invade your boundaries: a difficult boss, an unruly employee, maybe a peer that doesn't carry his or her weight. These are the things that are really challenging, and these are the things we need help with.

We've broken these problems down into very specific areas; whether it's a boss where we talk about managing up, an employee we talk about managing down, roles that people fall into. And we have a final category, which we call fatal attractions.

PM: I notice that you have a concept that the audience, I think, would benefit greatly from knowing about called *unhooking*. Can you talk about that?

KC: Gladly, Peter. When someone else's behavior really bothers you, whether it's the nasal tone in their voice or the fact that they may have just singled you out in a meeting and yelled at you, we actually get hooked. We churn up emotionally, and we obsess about the situation. It prevents us from doing our work well. If you can unhook, that is if you can take steps to change your internal reaction and then figure out the business actions available to you, then you change your result and you actually change the dynamic with the other person.

PM: In order to take the steps of first unhooking physically . . .

KC: Yes.

PM: . . . you take a deep breath and . . .

KC: Yes. Physically is the first thing. You have to cool the system down. Whether it is that you splash water on your face, take a deep breath, take a walk around the block, or even go work out, if something's really churning you up, that is the first step.

We follow that with mental unhooking, which is to look at your situation from a clear perspective. You have to ask yourself questions. What's going on here? What are the facts? What's their part? What's my part and what are my real options?

Finally we move into unhooking verbally. What are some of the things you can say to actually improve your situation? The other person's not going to change, but there's a way you can move it forward.

You can use unhooking as a business tool, which is anything from writing a memo or sending an e-mail to follow up on what you just said, to documenting someone else's behavior, to referring to policies and procedures.

PM: Unhooking mentally would be using the thinking part of your mind to connect up with the feeling part of your mind and verbalizing the fact that you know that you are feeling a certain way but doesn't mean you have to act it out.

KC: Yes.

PM: So therefore unhooking mentally may be, I know as bad as this feels to me the person who did that is in a world of pain, and it's not really personal to me, and I need to not respond personally.

PM: Right. Let me give you an example. When you're in a meeting and someone takes credit for an idea that you originally had, first you'd breathe and bring yourself back into the room and try to prevent yourself from wanting to kill that person. Then the mental unhooking would be to say to yourself, Okay, what just happened here? You know George just took credit for my idea. It is still my idea. There's a way that I can take it back. And so now I have to think of how I can do that.

PM: It would be, it would be more like well, taking the high road when, when, as you say, when I had this idea I presented it to everybody.

KC: That's . . .

PM: And not even arguing.

KC: That's right, Peter. Yeah. Taking the high road is a way to create a win-win. Taking the low road, which is to say, God, you took another one of my ideas, would be a way where there's a winner and a loser, and it really doesn't move you forward in your workplace situation.

When you're under stress it weakens your immune system. And we know of individuals when we do our consulting who go to work every day with a knot in their stomach or literally a pain in their neck, or their blood pressure begins to rise as they're approaching a situation. We all need tools; we need help in how to slow that process down, how to calm ourselves down so that we can really see the situation from a place where we feel as if we have choice. People often feel trapped at work. I'm trapped by my incompetent co-worker. I'm trapped by this demanding customer, and I don't know how to get out.

Keith Hammonds »

Editor of *Fast Company* magazine

PETER MORRIS: Our topic today is how to tame the alpha boss. Why don't you just share the four types of alpha bosses with us?

KEITH HAMMONDS: Sure. This came out of a firm called Worth Ethic in Austin, which did a survey of 1,500 business-people and came up with four categories. No one person is exactly just one category. But first is the commander, a guy like Jack Welch say. (I've got to be careful here; Jack Welch embodies some of these traits, and I'm not going to say that Jack Welch embodies all of the bad traits of the alpha boss.) The commander is energetic, decisive, motivating. But take these traits too far, push them over to the dark side, and the same boss can be a domineering, intimidating, very uncontrollable, abusive guy.

Next is the visionary. Our prototype is Richard Branson, head of Virgin Air. Ambitious, creative, really an example of inspirational guys at their best. On the dark side, these bosses can be overconfident, unrealistic, and defensive when challenged.

Number three, the strategist. Someone like Michael Eisner, ex-CEO of Disney. Intelligent, objective, someone highly analytical, problem-solver. The dark side can be smug, pretentious, and unemotional when approached.

PM: Okay. And the fourth category?

KH: Fourth, someone like Sam Walton: an executor. Someone very disciplined, demanding, tireless worker. He can also be more than demanding—impatient and unreasonable, and someone who doesn't appreciate the efforts of the people who work for him.

PM: The commander and the executor seem to have some overlap. Because I would say that Jack Welch definitely would be also an executor.

KH: Yeah, I think you can find overlap between all four. Jack Welch fits very nicely into the commander camp but he is also a tireless, disciplined, and demanding guy. Those are executor traits.

PM: Now let's talk about the visionary. It's really somebody that's brilliant in ideas and knows when to step aside and have some really tough people run it for him.

KH: Well, or he might not know to do that.

PM: And that's a lot of entrepreneurs who don't know when to get out of the way.

KH: Exactly.

PM: The strategist. If we were to look at a guy like Eisner, I think in a lot of ways he was viewed as a master manipulator who ran amok. Think of somebody so interested in moving people around that he loses his sight of the overall mission.

KH: Well, he's someone who thinks strategically. Who will think about five, ten years out? What is my course of action going to be? What's the plan? I think you make a great observation: The dark side of strategy is manipulation. And that's when we start treating people like chess pieces.

PM: I think these categories help how leadership functions and how people need to understand the pluses and minuses. So turn it on its side: What do you do as a senior manager reporting to one of these leaders? How do you help manage the downside?

KH: I think a lot depends on what your relationship with that person is. If you've got his or her trust, you've got to confront him or her.

PM: Is an intervention necessary where a group of people get together?

KH: You could do that. The reason there is a firm called Worth Ethic, consulting to companies like Dell, eBay, and Microsoft, is that this is very hard to do from the inside. Sometimes it takes an outsider, a strong outsider, to do the intervention.

More often than not, the executive isn't going to recognize his own weaknesses. You know it's going to take someone else in the organization. It could be the board of directors, if it's a CEO or chairman. It could be a peer. But it's got to be someone with a base of power in the organization.

PM: Worth Ethic has worked for Dell and Michael Dell gave a good recommendation about the company.

KH: Yeah.

PM: So in the case of Dell, do you think he called? Do you think is board nudged him? Or what do you think happened?

KH: I don't know for sure. I would guess that he did not. Michael Dell is not an extroverted executive, and I think what occurred was that he wasn't relating all that well to his subordinates. He didn't appreciate their work. So is he going to recognize something like that about himself and ask for help? I think the chances are not, but I don't know for sure.

PM: But somebody had to have a big stick to get him to deal with them then . . .

KH: Well, you know, hats off to Michael Dell. When someone pointed it out, he recognized that he's not perfect, he needs help and, yeah, he brought in some outsiders who could do the job.

Nan Mooney »

Author of *I Can't Believe She Did That!*
Why Women Betray Other Women at Work

PETER MORRIS: Welcome, Nan. Tell us what's unique about the way women betray women at work, since obviously it's not gender specific. Men betray men all the time. How is it different with women?

NAN MOONEY: One of the main differences is how we're raised. Men are usually raised to expect competition and to be comfortable with it in their personal relationships and to be very direct with each other when there is a conflict. Women get a lot of messages early on that the only good relationships with other women are the ones that are conflict-free, super supportive, super nice. And so we get into a competitive situation with one another or where a conflict arises and we don't know how to deal with it. We end up competing behind the other person's back. Competing in a way where it looks like we're not competing.

PM: And there is that kind of surreptitious more subtle derision and more divisive undercover conduct.

NM: That can be especially difficult because you don't know what you're dealing with. Did she really mean that? Are the rumors I hear that you're talking about me behind my back true? Whereas, if someone is directly having a problem with you and telling you, at least you know how to take step one to address it.

PM: So do you recommend that in all grade school courses throughout America that girls should be taught boxing?

NM: I think it's more in our personal relationships that we don't know how to deal with having conflicts. Because of course the relationships we have with our work colleagues are personal. They're not the same as private friendships but they're certainly not the same as being on a sports field either—they're somewhere in the middle. I think it is important that we start learning at an early age how to communicate about conflicts and about negative feelings.

PM: What message do you want to get across? Just that women need to train themselves culturally to be more direct and more confrontational?

NM: I think that is important. But I think that women in the workplace need to be more aware when these dynamics come up and to communicate with one another when there's a problem, even though it can feel dangerous. I think most of us know from experience the longer you sit on a problem and don't address it the worse it gets. So I think women need to learn to be a little braver about being direct when there's a conflict issue between them.

PM: Do you find that certain career paths and certain companies or jobs for women are more helpful to women becoming more direct?

NM: One interesting dynamic I came across is that there were very different interactions among women in environments that were still mostly male and where most of the power was still in the hands of men. There's sort of that feeling that there really isn't room for very many women. So women don't tend to be very generous and communicative with the other women working around them. They may even try to sabotage them or try to make them look bad. Whereas if you're in a situation where there are a lot of women working together then everyone's feeling so much pressure to be super nice and super supportive, they don't know how to raise a conflict without looking like the bad guy.

PM: Are you saying that women tend to be more underhanded because they're—

NM: Not more underhanded. In fact I would say, if anything, maybe the conflict in those situations tends to be more direct. But it's coming from a different place. It's coming from fear that there isn't room for enough women. Whereas, when you're in a situation where there are a lot of women working together, there isn't that fear. But that situation awakens a different fear, that if you raise conflict you're being a bad woman.

PM: Nan, can you share with us some anecdotes that are particularly telling about how these betrayals come about and what is the nature of them?

NM: Well, I'll tell you a personal one, which was what got me on the road to this subject. Shortly out of college I was working in Los Angeles. I was an assistant. I had another colleague who was an assistant to somebody else in the same office and we both figured out that there wasn't much room for us to move up. We talked a little about moving on.

I decided to make the move to leave, and I started looking for new jobs. She was asking me about it, and I was sharing information. She was very supportive, telling me, those sounds great, you should apply for this, all that sort of thing.

After a lot of searching I finally found a job that I thought would be really good for me and sent in my application. It was in New York so I flew back there to interview. Then I got a phone call telling me it's down to three people. One day, I walk into the office, and my colleague clears her throat and says, "I need to tell you something."

I said, "Okay."

She said, "I applied for that job, too. And I'm one of those three people it's down to."

And I was flabbergasted. Not by the fact that she had applied for the job too, but that she had been so secretive about it and never let on until it was impossible for her to hide it any longer. She had been pumping me for information. And I felt betrayed by her, by her lack of communication. I really felt like she'd taken advantage of me. And at that age, I had no idea how to deal with that.

PM: What would you say now, now that you've had all this experience?

NM: I think I would have been much more direct that I didn't think that that was a respectful way to deal with somebody.

PM: Now were you angry? Where you vindictive? Did you seek revenge?

NM: No, I felt like I had done something wrong. I was angry, but I felt, how stupid of me to share that information. I was angry at her as well. I think that I would not been so shocked if that had happened to a man, because I was more prepared in my mind for the fact that men are competitive in the workplace.

PM: And who got the job?

NM: Neither of us; the third person got it. So then we had to continue to work together with this having happened and neither of us knowing what to say about it or how to address it.

PM: Were you able, or were both of you able to repair the relationship or . . .

NM: No, we never said another word about it again.

Paul Babiak »

Author of *Snakes in Suits: When Psychopaths Go to Work*

PETER MORRIS: There's a lot of people who I would call *psycho* in laymen's terms who may be reasonably conscious and not delusional. On the other hand they generally are in denial and don't know how they come off to others.

PAUL BABIAK: Well someone who is psychopathic or has psychopathy has a personality disorder. And that's not mental illness. They're not delusional at all. They're quite perceptive and very much in control of the situation themselves, and they're very much aware. A personality disorder can be thought of as how one's mind, how one's personality is organized. These people happen to be organized around things like antisocial behavior; bullying is one possible characteristic. They're pathological liars. They are deceitful, dishonest people who lie, cheat, and steal. And they have no conscience. They know the difference between right and wrong but they find our distinction between the two quite amusing. They'll easily and quickly flip from one side to the other, as long as it gets them what they want.

    I like to think of these people as Dr. Jekyll and Mr. Hyde. They carry with them their personality disorder, these behaviors, everywhere they go. But they can choose what side they want to show to you. Certainly the first time they meet people, they present a very smooth, charming, glib, very entertaining, intelligent persona.

PM: That's the honeymoon phase.

PB: Absolutely, yes. While you're being enthralled by their surface, and you're growing to like them and beginning to trust them, they're analyzing you. They're trying to figure out what you have that they want and what they need to do to get it. That glides under the radar; that's hidden. Over time they establish a bond, we call it the psychopathic bond, between themselves and you, and they move in from the from the assessment phase to the manipulation phase.

Here's where they begin to use things that in business we might call impression management techniques to get things from individuals that they need and want. These could be money and sex, things like that. Or they could be something like prestige, status, even information that they'll use to get other things from other individuals. But once you've been caught in the psychopathic web, you often don't see the harmful nature of it. In fact, you're more than willing to help out your buddy—who happens to be a psychopath.

Finally, there's the third phase we label abandonment. This happens when the psychopath decides you don't have anything more for them, and they just leave you cold. They literally either walk away or they just stop calling and they don't respond. It's as if you don't exist and never did. This is often shocking to people who've fallen into this bonding, this psychopathic fiction. Only at that point do you realize that the person you've been dealing with is not a real person—they're a fictional character that's been constructed just to manipulate you.

PM: If somebody finds a psychopath in the workplace that they're working with, is there anyway to continue a working relationship albeit with extreme caution?

PB: I think that's dangerous, because if the psychopath has been on the job in the organization for a good amount of time, they've established a power network. They've extended the psychopathic fiction to numerous people in the organization. So unbeknownst to you they may have established relationships with people over you and maybe much higher over you in the organization. Should you ever cross them, confront them, or if they suspect that you've figured out what their scam is, they'll pull some strings, make some phone calls, and you could find yourself out of a job. So it's a dangerous game.

PM: So you really advise people to either blow the whistle or get out or move over and transfer, but not to stay there.

PB: If you've been identified by the psychopath as a target. Then you have something of value to them, and they'll play along with you as long as you allow yourself to be manipulated. Once you realize you're being conned and you want to change the situation, that's when the bullying and some of the violence can take place. At that point I would look to transfer to another position in the organization. I might even consider a totally different job.

As far as blowing the whistle, I would make sure I understand the HR policies in the organization before I do that. I would contact them but I would probably do it anonymously at first or use whatever hotline the organization might have to bring information to their attention. It's best to bring data. If you have financial reports that have been doctored, they need to see a copy of that. Perhaps they need to do an internal audit. Bring in a fraud investigator.

There are three kinds of psychopaths. The first is the manipulator or the con. This is the person who does a lot of talking and uses his voice and his or her voice and intelligence to manipulate people, usually verbally.

The second type is the bully. That tends to be someone who may not be as sophisticated or educated, who tends to use more intimidation and overt force, either physical or often just a loud yelling and screaming approach.

Third is what we call the puppet master. The puppet master has more of the traits and characteristics of a psychopath than the other two do. They'll manipulate people directly reporting to them, who they have power over, getting those people to do their dirty work.

PM: Is it almost impossible to educate, train, cure, or ameliorate an adult who has a condition that would be considered psychopathic?

PB: Yes. In general society we know that one in a hundred people has psychopathy as a personality disorder. If you travel, and I'm sure you do, I'm sure you meet a hundred people in any given day. So you run the risk of at least meeting one psychopath in a regular day. In prison, we find 15 percent of the population are psychopaths. Scientists did research on them and found that when they went through the therapy they came out and got higher psychopathy scores. It made them better psychopaths.

PM: They learn how to fake being healthy.

PB: You got it. As people emote and as they talk in the therapy group, the psychopath is making mental notes, and they're able to mimic these emotions later on, and therefore it goes into their arsenal of tools to be used when they want to manipulate people. Let's say a psychopath wants to come across as contrite, as expressing regret and remorse. They now have a better picture of what that looks like to the rest of us.

Rosabeth Kanter »

Author of *Confidence: How Winning Streaks and Losing Streaks Begin and End*

PETER MORRIS: I'm delighted to say hello Rosabeth Kanter and fascinated by your great achievements and about the subject of confidence in your new book, *Confidence: How Winning Streaks and Losing Streaks Begin and End.*

ROSABETH KANTER: Thank you very much. I'm talking about a kind of leader and a kind of company that builds confidence because they don't treat their people as disposable.

PM: That's well put. And the art of treating people as not disposable I assume relates to a lot of investment and training, mentorship, coaching, leading, setting goals, holding accountability, and working collaboratively.

RK: Absolutely, all of those things. But there's something else that I saw in not only in business but in all the great sports teams in countries, any place where there is the ability to keep succeeding time and time again. There were not only the investments in the people side; leaders themselves believed that people have the potential to achieve.

One of the great arts of leadership is to build confidence in advance of victory. You know it's easy when you're already winning to say, oh yeah, we've got really good people. But it's those leaders that were able to turn around losing situations, declining situations, that really impress me. Like Jim Kilts at Gillette, who turned around Gillette and then sold it to Procter & Gamble for a lot of money, or Gordon Bethune who turned about Continental Airlines, or Nelson Mandela who turned about South Africa, or the people at the New England Patriots or the Philadelphia Eagles who turned around their franchises. They all believed in human talent and that's why they made those investments.

PM: They also view success as not monolithic and not a one-shot deal, but a marathon more than a sprint. They are able to embrace the ambivalence of what you call the middle.

RK: Thank you for mentioning that because this is really helpful to me. I defined what I call Kanter's Law: Everything can look like a failure in the middle. Anything that we begin to undertake, whether it's a new venture, a new product, construction on our home, there is always ahead of us more obstacles, potential trouble, and knowing that we could get through it. Confidence is the ability to believe that success is possible. In those companies that have built a great deal of confidence in their people, people believe they can do anything. They can perform miracles. They can get through any crisis. Those companies are more likely to bounce back from troubles.

Sharon Armstrong»

Author of *Stress-Free Performance Appraisals*

PETER MORRIS: I'm dying to have you explain the seeming contradiction between "stress free" on one hand and "performance appraisal" on the other.

SHARON ARMSTRONG: Yeah, I've been accused of using an oxymoron. But I think it can be stress-free if you follow some simple techniques. There are definitely some things managers can do to make sure they are making this stress-free.

It's part of the manager's job to make sure that the review's contents isn't a surprise. They should have been talking about performance appraisal and performance evaluation the entire cycle. That starts at the very beginning of the cycle, with planning goals and then having a number of meetings and conversations throughout the cycle to review progress so that the employee will really be aware of how they're being assessed.

PM: In general, that form of emotional hygiene in the workplace is very advisable, and I agree with you.

SA: The manager's gotten to know the employee. He's trying to create an environment that will engage and motivate that employee and kept in touch. And really that means talking all the time so that when the time for the appraisal meeting happens, it's just summarizing all those other discussions.

PM: What are the ingredients of a stress-free performance appraisal?

SA: Starting the meeting in a professional way. Making sure there is that back and forth discussion throughout the performance appraisal. Closing it in a professional way and then doing any follow-up.

I would give you five hallmarks in addition to that preparation. One, there is a good attitude on the part of the supervisor. Two, you can actually get the employee to talk, to be an active participant. Three, there's mutual problem-solving. Four, mutual goal-setting. And last, the appraisal should be packed with examples: last March you did that, last summer these three activities. Nothing makes it more real than those examples.

Goal-setting is key. Looking forward to see what the department is going be doing that's hopefully aligned with the organization's strategic plan and the value that employee has to add. I wouldn't spend a lot of time looking back, but spending a portion of the time looking forward.

PM: Yes. That all makes sense. Now share with us, what are some of the common errors made in a performance appraisal?

SA: There's one big one that happens; it's called recency. It's when you get distracted by something that happened two weeks before you sit down with the employee, and that's all you can remember. It becomes bigger than life, and you don't look over the entire evaluation cycle. People do have a tendency to think about what happened recently, especially if they're not keeping good notes throughout the cycle.

Another pitfall we can fall into when we're appraising is called the *halo effect*. This is where there's one particular good aspect someone shows in their job that takes on bigger-than-life appearance the employer. So the whole rating is good as a result of that one thing. (The opposite is the *horns effect*.) These are good things to avoid.

PM: That sounds simpler than it probably is to execute. Of course, a grievance procedure would occur if the employee feels unheard or unfairly tagged with things that the appraiser is unwilling to listen to or correct or adjust in the interview.

SA: Yeah. And I think you can avoid going down that road, if you're doing the work ahead of time. All the things that we just mentioned—if you have those in place

people will feel, hopefully, they might not agree with
the review but you can talk it over and do something
about it.

PM: Sharon, are there ever appraisals where the employees
are evaluating their bosses face-to-face?

SA: Yeah, there are. In fact, I included that in my book,
a sample upward appraisal. I love the idea. I think it
should be done for development reasons, 'cause who
best knows how we supervise than our direct reports?
But you have to build some safeguards into the process.

PM: But that's generally not mandatory or practiced regularly
in business today, the upward appraisals.

SA: I haven't seen much of it, Peter. I wish there was more.
Some companies are doing a three-sixty-degree feedback. This is feedback that comes from all directions:
above, below, and on all sides. That is starting to come
into more and more companies. And I hope that does
continue to grow.

PM: Yes, and I couldn't agree more. What are some of the
challenges that your clients have come to you with in
executing on the programs that you've given them?
Can you share that with us?

SA: Sure. I think one issue, one challenge that companies
have is they expect managers to be able to do performance appraisals without training. I did a lot of interviews for my book, and I asked managers, what makes
this so difficult? They told me they were never taught
how, it makes them uncomfortable, they're afraid it's
going be misunderstood, they don't have the time, the
situation isn't serious, they don't want to make a big
deal of it. . . . All these excuses, and they weren't held
accountable for doing feedback throughout the year and
having a good performance appraisal discussion. I think
that has to change. I think companies have the responsibility to make sure they're not only setting up good

systems, but also giving managers the support to really
be able to implement that system.

PM: Yes. And that really goes back to the rubric of what I
like to call *good mental hygiene,* that it's important to do
this regularly and professionally. And if you do that and
you stay current with your obligation then you move
into the land of the stress-free, and that's . . .

SA: I think that's right. You set up systems for yourself that
work with you. There's no cookie-cutter approach to
how to do that. I think each manager has his or her own
style and way to manage and just have to build into that
system, having these conversations and tracking notes so
you'll have material to put in a good appraisal at the end
of the cycle.

PM: Yes. And I think this is all very good advice. Now there
are some companies that you mention in your book
that have appraisals that are done in a little different way,
like the National Cooperative Bank. Can you give us an
example of something that's a little different?

SA: Yes, this is a local D.C.-based bank, a financial services
company. Their appraisal is all employee-driven. I'm
seeing more of this happening. The employee starts the
process. This really brings home that this is a partnership, and it's really about the employee and their career.
So they start the process. They pull their goals together.
They pull their results. They gather objective information regarding their performance from other people
they worked with through the year. They fill out a self-
assessment. Only then do they go to their supervisor to
get ready for the performance appraisal.

PM: So the employee has the role and the responsibility of
instigating the assessment and comes forward with self-
assessment first?

SA: Yep. And all the documentation about what goals he
and the supervisor set and how well he or she had

done. Now, the supervisor will certainly be able to edit and comment. There'll be a real discussion. But a lot of that work falls on the employee rather than on the supervisor.

PM: Of course, all of this is predicated on having reasonably healthy emotionally and psychologically oriented supervisors and subordinates. How do you handle somebody where you end up with a psycho or someone who's a little bit crazy?

SA: Well, let's take it from the first point, if the employee just kind of goes berserk and they take no responsibility for the behavior. I terminate that meeting immediately. Because that's not the type of setting in which you want to try to discuss performance. You set up ground rules for the next time.

I think it's dicier when an employee is faced with a boss who flies off the handle. I think we've all been in situations where we've left bosses, we haven't left jobs.

Timothy Wilson》

Author of *Strangers to Ourselves: Discovering the Adaptive Unconscious*

PETER MORRIS: Good to have you here, Timothy Wilson. Share with us the core premise of your book *Strangers to Ourselves: Discovering the Adaptive Unconscious.*

TIMOTHY WILSON: Well, I think there's been a revolution in psychology in the last several years in how we view unconscious thinking. Unconscious thinking used to be viewed from a Freudian perspective in which it was this dark beast-in-the-basement that everyone wanted to keep at bay and do our best to avoid thinking about. But the modern view is that actually a great deal of our mental processing occurs unconsciously, and it's a good thing that it does. We have very powerful brains that are able to size up the world, analyze it, size up other people in ways that we don't even know we're doing. So in a nutshell, my book is about this new kind of unconscious thinking, the implications of that for self-knowledge and things like that.

PM: What you're saying is there's a new perception of a way of thinking that's obviously been there but hasn't been understood or packaged so to speak into common knowledge.

TW: Well I suppose. Sometimes the best way to solve problems is not to sit down and take out a piece of paper and make a list of plus and minuses and really analyze it. In fact, that sometimes can be the worst thing to do because it muddles us and it's better at times to let our unconscious do the thinking.

PM: The whole dichotomy between thinking and feeling is so critical and there are many people, me included, who grew up learning to use our verbal skills and trained in logic analysis and only as we get more experienced and learn about ourselves and make enough mistakes do we begin to realize that often the best voice we hear is the voice that comes when we least expect it, it comes, it flows from the unconscious.

TW: Yes.

PM: And that's the point isn't it?

TW: The hard question is when to listen to that voice. I wouldn't want to oversimplify this to say that the unconscious always provides a better answer.

PM: I agree.

TW: In fact, I think one of the best pieces of advice that I can give you is to not only to listen to that voice but to control the information we give to our unconscious. The unconscious is very good at combining and sifting through information, but it's only as good as the information we give it. I think in a lot of business decisions, for example, the danger we can get into is saying well, it doesn't matter if I input some good or bad data, I'll be able to tell the good from the bad and tell whether my judgment's biased or not. But once that information gets into our unconscious, it rattles around in there, and out comes a judgment. It might well be biased if we've given it false data.

PM: I like to say to people that I work with that intuition without research is gun slinging.

TW: Excellent. That's great.

PM: How can we can get more in touch with our unconscious in the constructive way that you talk about?

TW: I'm not a big fan of introspection. I don't think that we can just stare inward and suddenly the door's open and we have a direct view of our own conscious processing, anymore than we can stare at the wires of our computer and figure out what our computer's doing. I think we have to look at ourselves as an outsider would and watch what we do and watch our patterns of behavior and try to deduce our own conscious processing. And that's not easy.

PM: Well I do agree that it's very difficult to be able to step back and look at yourself objectively and to look at and feel your emotions on one hand but not be driven by them, and then make decisions.

TW: Yeah. I think another approach is to pay attention to what other people think of us. That's not to say that they're always right and we're wrong when we disagree. But I do think that if we're in a situation where there's a pretty unanimous opinion of our friends and colleagues that we have a problem, we should realize we might have a problem. And, you know, this is formalized of course in some business settings with three-sixty evaluations where you do this formally and that can be a painful process to have to read and see about what other people are saying about us candidly. But if we can at least open our minds to seeing ourselves through the eyes of others that can often be a good exercise.

PM: Of course, like everything in life there's a balance. If we get too caught up in that we stop being genuine and we start trying to affect others and shortcut that process.

       The other thing I would say is that if we think positive and do positive and feel positive, it does reinforce itself. And if we do generous things we feel generous, we become generous, and it becomes a positive cycle as opposed to doing things of a negative cycle.

TW: I think that's true. Some people are better at bringing out the good side in us than others, and those are the treasured friends I think.

       It's interesting what you say about different people bringing different things out of us because I do think we tend to view ourselves as one static personality that is the same from situation to situation. But as you suggest, I think that can be quite different from one relationship to the next.

PM: Do you have any interesting case studies of people that
      you work with or observed who've grown and been
      able to better hear their unconscious and work with it?

TW: I think we can all think of people we know who per-
      haps have a bit of a tin ear for feedback from others.
      They're very rigid people who are inflexible from one
      situation to the next. Just being able to take that step
      back, even doubting your own judgment sometimes and
      saying, I view the situation one way but others view it
      another way and maybe I should at least question my
      own view. Not that I should always adopt other peoples'
      views but at least question my own way of thinking.

references

Books and Magazine Articles

Armstrong, Sharon, and Madelyn Appelbaum. 2003. *Stress-free Performance Appraisals: Turn Your Most Painful Management Duty into a Powerful Motivational Tool.* Franklin Lakes, NJ: Career Press.

Babiak, Paul, and Robert D. Hare. 2007. *Snakes in Suits: When Psychopaths Go to Work.* New York: HarperCollins.

Branham, F. Leigh. 2000. *Keeping the People Who Keep You in Business.* New York: AMACOM/American Management Association.

Cohen, Ben, and Mal Warwick. 2006. *Values-Driven Business.* San Francisco: Berrett-Koehler Publishers.

Collins, Jim. 2001. *Good to Great: Why Some Companies Make the Leap . . . And Others Don't.* New York: HarperCollins.

Crowley, Katherine, and Kathi Elster. 2007. *Working with You Is Killing Me: Freeing Yourself from Emotional Traps at Work.* New York: Warner Business Books.

Drucker, Peter F. 2001. *Management Challenges for the 21st Century.* New York: HarperCollins.

Feiner, Michael. 2005. *The Feiner Points of Leadership.*
New York: Warner Business Books.

Friedman, Caitlin, and Kimberly Yorio. 2006. *The Girl's Guide to Being a Boss (Without Being a Bitch).* New York: Broadway Books.

Goleman, Dan. 1998. *Working with Emotional Intelligence.*
New York: Bantam Books.

Hammonds, Keith. May 2006. "Taming the Alpha Exec."
Fast Company magazine.

Kanter, Rosabeth Moss. 2006. *Confidence: How Winning Streaks and Losing Streaks Begin and End.* New York: Three Rivers Press.

Kotter, John P. 1996. *Leading Change.* Boston: Harvard Business School Press.

McGregor, Douglas. 1960. *The Human Side of Enterprise.*
New York: McGraw-Hill.

Mendlin, Ronald, and Marc Polonsky. 2000. *The "Double You."* Indianapolis: Jist Works.

Menkes, Justin. 2005. *Executive Intelligence: What All Great Leaders Have.* New York: HarperCollins.

Mooney, Nan. 2005. *I Can't Believe She Did That! Why Women Betray Other Women at Work.* New York: St. Martin's/Griffin.

Polonsky, Ph.D, Ira. 1994–2005. *Mental Fitness.* Professional Health Plan Publications (Self-published monograph).

Random House Webster's College Dictionary. 2000. New York: Random House Reference.

Senge, Peter. 1994. *The Fifth Discipline*. New York: Currency Doubleday.

Thrower, Mitch. 2005. *The Attention-Deficit Workplace: Winning Strategies for Success in Today's Fast-Paced Business Environment*. Guilford, CT: Lyons Press.

Topchik, Gary. 2001. *Managing Workplace Negativity*. New York: AMACOM/American Management Association.

Wilson, Timothy. 2002. *Strangers to Ourselves: Discovering the Adaptive Unconscious*. Boston: Belknap Press.

Wolaner, Robin. 2005. *Naked in the Boardroom: A CEO Bares Her Secrets So You Can Transform Your Career*. New York: Fireside, Simon & Schuster.

Web Articles "Bathing a Newborn Buddha." *www.serve.com/cmtan/ buddhism/Treasure/bathing.newborn.html*.

"Competition: How Hypnosis Can Help Women to Hold Their Own in the Workplace." *www.findarticles. com/p/articles/mi_qa4087/is_200407/ai_n9425395/pg_3*.

"Functioning Amid Dysfunction: Coping with Conflict at the Office." *www.careerjournal.com/myc/officelife/ 20060905-schaefer.html*.

"Handling a Boss Who Has Turned on You." *http://love. ivillage.com/fnf/fnfwork/0,,23jb,00.html*.

"Handling a Boss Who Works Short Hours." *http:// weblog.infoworld.com/lewis/archives/2006/03/handling_a_ boss.html*.

"How to Handle a Boss Who Takes Credit for Your Work." *www.careerjournal.com/myc/climbing/20060816-schaefer.html*.

"How Suite It Isn't: A Dearth of Female Bosses." *New York Times*. December 17, 2006. *www.nytimes.com/2006/12/17/business/yourmoney/17csuite.html?_r=1&oref=slogin*.

"Information on Sexual Harassment." *www.de2.psu.edu/harassment/generalinfo/*.

"Mental Hygiene." *The Columbia Encyclopedia*, Sixth Edition. 2001–2005. *www.bartleby.com/65/me/mentalhy.html*.

"Now It's Time for Women to Get Even." *Washington Post* column *Life at Work*, April 23, 2006. *www.washingtonpost.com/wp-dyn/content/article/2006/04/22/AR2006042200134.html*.

"The Origin of the Handshake." *http://soc302.tripod.com/soc_302rocks/id8.html*.

"Poor Management Responsible for Negative Productivity." *www.teamlmi.com/news/latest/poor-management-responsible-for-negative-productivity.html*.

"Tips on Handling a Bully of a Boss." *www.careerjournal.com/myc/officelife/20060928-schaefer.html?cjcontent=m*.

"What Is Title IX?" *www.american.edu/sadker/titleix.htm*.

"What the Wage Gap Doesn't Show Us." CNN.com column *Everyday Money*. *http://money.cnn.com/2006/02/21/commentary/everyday/sahadi/index.htm*.

index

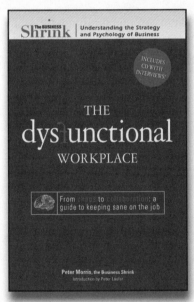
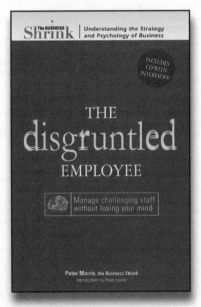

Software License Agreement

YOU SHOULD CAREFULLY READ THE FOLLOWING TERMS AND CONDITIONS BEFORE USING THIS SOFTWARE PRODUCT. INSTALLING AND USING THIS PRODUCT INDICATES YOUR ACCEPTANCE OF THESE CONDITIONS. IF YOU DO NOT AGREE WITH THESE TERMS AND CONDITIONS, DO NOT INSTALL THE SOFTWARE AND RETURN THIS PACKAGE PROMPTLY FOR A FULL REFUND.

1. Grant of License
This software package is protected under United States copyright law and international treaty. You are hereby entitled to one copy of the enclosed software and are allowed by law to make one backup copy or to copy the contents of the disks onto a single hard disk and keep the originals as your backup or archival copy. United States copyright law prohibits you from making a copy of this software for use on any computer other than your own computer. United States copyright law also prohibits you from copying any written material included in this software package without first obtaining the permission of F+W Publications, Inc.

2. Restrictions
You, the end-user, are hereby prohibited from the following:
You may not rent or lease the Software or make copies to rent or lease for profit or for any other purpose.
You may not disassemble or reverse compile for the purposes of reverse engineering the Software.
You may not modify or adapt the Software or documentation in whole or in part, including, but not limited to, translating or creating derivative works.

3. Transfer
You may transfer the Software to another person, provided that (a) you transfer all of the Software and documentation to the same transferee; (b) you do not retain any copies; and (c) the transferee is informed of and agrees to the terms and conditions of this Agreement.

4. Termination
This Agreement and your license to use the Software can be terminated without notice if you fail to comply with any of the provisions set forth in this Agreement. Upon termination of this Agreement, you promise to destroy all copies of the software including backup or archival copies as well as any documentation associated with the Software. All disclaimers of warranties and limitation of liability set forth in this Agreement shall survive any termination of this Agreement.

5. Limited Warranty
F+W Publications, Inc. warrants that the Software will perform according to the manual and other written materials accompanying the Software for a period of 30 days from the date of receipt. F+W Publications, Inc. does not accept responsibility for any malfunctioning computer hardware or any incompatibilities with existing or new computer hardware technology.

6. Customer Remedies
F+W Publications, Inc.'s entire liability and your exclusive remedy shall be, at the option of F+W Publications, Inc., either refund of your purchase price or repair and/or replacement of Software that does not meet this Limited Warranty. Proof of purchase shall be required. This Limited Warranty will be voided if Software failure was caused by abuse, neglect, accident or misapplication. All replacement Software will be warranted based on the remainder of the warranty or the full 30 days, whichever is shorter and will be subject to the terms of the Agreement.

7. No Other Warranties
F+W PUBLICATIONS, INC., TO THE FULLEST EXTENT OF THE LAW, DISCLAIMS ALL OTHER WARRANTIES, OTHER THAN THE LIMITED WARRANTY IN PARAGRAPH 5, EITHER EXPRESS OR IMPLIED, ASSOCIATED WITH ITS SOFTWARE, INCLUDING BUT NOT LIMITED TO IMPLIED WARRANTIES OF MERCHANTABILITY AND FITNESS FOR A PARTICULAR PURPOSE, WITH REGARD TO THE SOFTWARE AND ITS ACCOMPANYING WRITTEN MATERIALS. THIS LIMITED WARRANTY GIVES YOU SPECIFIC LEGAL RIGHTS. DEPENDING UPON WHERE THIS SOFTWARE WAS PURCHASED, YOU MAY HAVE OTHER RIGHTS.

8. Limitations on Remedies
TO THE MAXIMUM EXTENT PERMITTED BY LAW, F+W PUBLICATIONS, INC. SHALL NOT BE HELD LIABLE FOR ANY DAMAGES WHATSOEVER, INCLUDING WITHOUT LIMITATION, ANY LOSS FROM PERSONAL INJURY, LOSS OF BUSINESS PROFITS, BUSINESS INTERRUPTION, BUSINESS INFORMATION OR ANY OTHER PECUNIARY LOSS ARISING OUT OF THE USE OF THIS SOFTWARE.
This applies even if F+W Publications, Inc. has been advised of the possibility of such damages. F+W Publications, Inc.'s entire liability under any provision of this agreement shall be limited to the amount actually paid by you for the Software. Because some states may not allow for this type of limitation of liability, the above limitation may not apply to you.
THE WARRANTY AND REMEDIES SET FORTH ABOVE ARE EXCLUSIVE AND IN LIEU OF ALL OTHERS, ORAL OR WRITTEN, EXPRESS OR IMPLIED. No F+W Publications, Inc. dealer, distributor, agent, or employee is authorized to make any modification or addition to the warranty.

9. General
This Agreement shall be governed by the laws of the United States of America and the Commonwealth of Massachusetts. If you have any questions concerning this Agreement, contact F+W Publications, Inc., via Adams Media at 508-427-7100. Or write to us at: Adams Media, an F+W Publications Company, 57 Littlefield Street, Avon, MA 02322.